Emotional CORE
THERAPY
FOR ADOLESCENTS

Robert Moylan

Copyright © 2012 Robert Moylan

All rights reserved.

ISBN: 1478160144

ISBN 13: 9781478160144

CONTENTS

Disclaimer.................................... V

Acknowledgements IX

Author's Note................................. XI

Introduction................................... 1

1.) How ECT Works............................. 17

2.) Using ECT to Treat Depression............. 45

3.) Using ECT to Treat Anxiety................ 73

4.) Using ECT to Understand Anger 97

5.) Using ECT to Help Couples................ 115

6.) ECT for Advanced Adolescents............. 137

DISCLAIMER

This book details the author's personal experiences with and opinions about mental health and relationships. The author and publisher are providing this book and its contents on an "as is" basis and make no representations or warranties of any kind with respect to this book or its contents. The author and publisher disclaim all such representations and warranties of merchantability and healthcare for a particular purpose. In addition, the author and publisher do not represent or warrant that the information accessible via this book is accurate, complete, or current.

The statements made in this book are not intended to diagnose, treat, cure, or prevent any specific condition or illness. Please consult with your own physician or mental healthcare provider regarding the suggestions and recommendations made in this book.

Neither the author nor the publisher will be liable for any damages arising out of, or in connection with the use of this book. This is a comprehensive limitation of liability that applies to damages of any kind, including (without limitation): compensatory, direct, indirect, or consequential damages; loss of data, income or profit, loss of or damage to property and claims of third parties.

You understand that this book is not intended as a substitute for consultation with a licensed healthcare practitioner, such as your physician or therapist. Before you begin any healthcare program or change your lifestyle in any way, you will consult with your physician or healthcare provider to ensure that you are in good health and that the examples used in this book will not harm you.

This book provides content related to mental health and relationships. As such, your use of this book implies your acceptance of this disclaimer.

Emotional CORE THERAPY

A Simple and Effective Method

to Empower the Mind

by

Robert A. Moylan, LCPC

ACKNOWLEDGEMENTS

I would like to thank my daughter, Anna, who brings me great joy. Also, a special thanks to my editor, Mike Valentino. His patience and expertise were invaluable during the writing of this book.

AUTHOR'S NOTE

The goal of this book is to show you how to live life to its fullest, without any regrets. But how can you do that when debilitating feelings of fear and grief continuously pop up to block your way? Like rain that falls no matter how much we want it to be a sunny day, fear and grief are an inevitable part of life that we cannot stop. Of course, that doesn't mean we can't protect ourselves from it! Realizing the potential for harm – and stopping it in its tracks – is a sure sign that you are a smart person who wants to stay healthy. You prepare for rain by carrying an umbrella. In a thunderstorm, you take cover in a shelter. In a tornado or hurricane, you go underground for added protection. Why not be just as protective with your emotional health? Be prepared for all scenarios. If it is a torrential downpour (best friend moves away, your boyfriend or girlfriend cheats on you, or you get kicked off the soccer team) why not get protection? There are powerful ways to accomplish this – you just have to access it. Therapists can help you release the emotional pain that comes with loss. ECT for Adolescents is a resource, just like an umbrella, shelter, etc. that also serves as a form of protection. The key is learning to release these feelings and loving and respecting yourself.

This book teaches you a simple easy to follow approach that will bring you one step closer to mastering your mind. The ECT Flowchart that you see on the adjacent page will be placed throughout the book at the end of each chapter. This will be beneficial for those visual learners who want to monitor their growth and progress in order to measure how much you have learned about the ECT process. A simple suggestion would be to use a highlighter or black marker at the end of each chapter to note which sections of the ECT flowchart you are able to comprehend.

A great way to learn psychology techniques is through storytelling. This book will utilize that approach as it makes learning the process of Emotional Core Therapy even simpler and more enjoyable. For readers who learn through a more interactive style, there will be a list of important concepts at the end of each chapter.

AUTHOR'S NOTE

5 Step ECT Flow Chart

Relationships;
self, other people, places, things

Four Authentic Feelings;
joy, grief, fear, relief

Uncomfortable Symptoms;
muscle tightness, fatigue, etc.

Releasing Process;
learn to discharge toxic feelings

Balancing Your Equilibrium;
practice various daily meditative techniques

INTRODUCTION

This book is about you. Yes, we're all individuals and we have plenty of differences, but what you'll learn here applies to all of us regardless of age, gender or anything else that sometimes separates people. That's because every single one of us, at one point or another will struggle with problems. But if you don't know how to properly deal with them, things can quickly go from bad to worse. Emotional Core Therapy (ECT) will show you a better way for handling your problems and having a happier life. As a therapist I've been using it very successfully for many years. What's even cooler is that you can learn how to use it to help yourself.

My approach to therapy is to first make sure that people realize that an anguished mind is every bit as painful (sometimes more so) than a hurting body. You would of course go to the doctor if you had a broken leg or a sore throat, right? But for some reason when it comes to the mind people (teenagers especially) are either embarrassed to admit that they have a problem, or worried that it won't work for them.

It doesn't have to be that way. There is no shame in seeking out help. In fact, it is courageous. Will treatment work? Well, in using Emotional Core Therapy, I've come to understand that there is no one "right way" to do therapy. There are lots of great therapists out there, utilizing a wide variety of highly innovative and successful techniques. If I tried to teach all of them, however, it would be overwhelming for the patient. ECT introduces a group of techniques that are simple to do, and they work over time. More importantly, it empowers people to help themselves. If I could teach you the perfect baseball swing, but you could only do it when I am right there standing next to you, what good would that do for you? By the same token, what good is therapy if it doesn't work when you leave the therapist's office? That is a basic premise that I always keep in mind when teaching people about the power that all of us have within ourselves to release our pain and to feel better. ECT has a primary goal of making sure that you can live a life of freedom and independence.

By learning to monitor their feelings, people can find out what has "hurt" them in life. The basic premise of ECT is to learn from each time that we have debilitating feelings of fear and loss. Let's look at something so simple as putting on a jacket on a cold and blustery day. To protect yourself from the cold, you have to put on layers of clothes to keep warm. I'm sure we all learned that at a young age. In ECT, we do something very similar with our feelings. Harmful feelings of fear and loss can actually endanger your body in much the same way that a snowy and wintry day would surely beat up on you if you dressed only in a T-shirt and shorts.

INTRODUCTION

The goal of ECT is to reduce toxic pain. By the time you finish reading this book you will be so familiar with the process that you will be able to use it whenever you need, just like slipping on that winter jacket whenever the temperature drops. At the heart of Emotional Core Therapy is learning how to identify and process the four authentic feelings that arise from all relationships. They are joy, grief, fear, and relief.

These things are universal to the entire human family. There is no problem in the world that someone else has not experienced. Emotional Core Therapy offers a practical, realistic and very effective method for dealing with all of them. It all begins with honoring your five senses: hearing, seeing, smelling, tasting and touching. Pay close attention to all five of them. What are they telling you? You will never really know if you impair your senses with toxins such as caffeine, drugs, alcohol, lack of sleep, etc. An individual who honors his or senses will be more aware not only of the outside world, but of their own inner world as well.

I like to use metaphors. They've been invaluable in forming my understanding of the world in assisting those who come to me for help. I will use them throughout this book. One of my favorites involves golf. A golfer needs to be honest with himself/herself, and decide if their emotions on the course are helping or hurting them. For example, would an aspiring pro golfer who throws his clubs when he misses a drive, be an improved golfer if he handled his emotions properly? Can the proper understanding of emotions lower your score? How many shots does one throw away because of poorly handled emotions? Mastering the psychology of the mind is essential for any amateur or professional golfer who strives to be his best. The idea is to truly be comfortable with one's self as well as learn to identify feelings that are uncomfortable, but sometimes things get a bit more complex.

Let me explain. Consider a golfer that hits four to five excellent shots in a row. To the naked eye, no problem, he is playing well, so he will want to keep the positive vibrations going. Right? Wrong, that is not what the elite golfers do! If they do, they will elevate their central nervous system, and before you know it they will make an errant shot from too much adrenaline. That is why, to the contrary, elite golfers have a calmness about them. Most have learned to maintain a good, balanced psyche. It is also important to realize that it is possible to have too many feelings of joy and relief.

But learning how to process our true feelings and properly handle our emotions not only goes well beyond golf, it actually applies to virtually all of life. Think about it, even without a major crisis, on a day in, day out basis we all have minor psychic pain of one sort or another. It could be a difficult to live with parent, a boss with a short fuse, a girlfriend or boyfriend who is always "pushing your buttons," etc. Though not debilitating, these daily irritants can build up and steal away your happiness and peace of mind. As you become more aware of your feelings, you will be better able to decide what

INTRODUCTION

you can handle and what you cannot. It may need to involve terminating certain relationships. For example, if a boss is so overbearing that you are living in misery, the only solution might be to find a new job. But there are also other techniques that can be used for identifying and releasing feelings, as we will see.

Of course, you have to use prudence and common sense too. If at any point you ever feel that you might be a danger to yourself or other people, you need to either call 911 or immediately check into a hospital Emergency Room. Though common and universal to all people, normally mild ailments such as sadness, anxiety and anger can sometimes be serious enough to require hospitalization. In every situation, err on the side of caution, as it's always better to be safe than sorry.

To help explain the many benefits of Emotional Core Therapy I want for you to imagine a rudderless rowboat rowing down the river. What does it take for a rowboat to traverse down the waterway? Fuel of course. In this case, fuel would consist of a healthy diet. By that we mean not using stimulants such as coffee, caffeinated soda, and excess sugar, all of which affect the central nervous system. All stimulants or depressants affect the four authentic feelings of joy, grief, fear, and relief. Minor uses such as a cup of coffee in the morning or salt on your popcorn, likely would not affect a person's central nervous system in a chronic manner. The best advice I can give here is to speak with your family doctor if you have concerns with your dietary intake. The important factor to remember is that food and drink can have a positive or negative impact on your central nervous system. Although the topic of food intake is beyond the scope of this book, just keep in mind that the relationship exists.

Back to our rudderless rowboat…it's gliding through the water effortlessly and smoothly. Try and visualize the peaceful state of the rowboat as it courses downstream. Soft, tranquil yet very sturdy. Quite a vessel, wouldn't you say? Now imagine if this rudderless rowboat was able to traverse the sea and ocean for months and years in the same manner. What an enjoyable experience. This is ideally, the emotional state of a person who has successfully learned ECT. Even if a person never read a word about ECT, they could have this same feeling. How? By just staying emotionally balanced and healthy their whole lives. Sounds like a fun and enjoyable way of life. So what is so hard about achieving this state? Rather than give you the answer, let's realistically explore what happens to people as they experience life using the rudderless rowboat example.

Now, with our rowboat traveling the waterways, what happens from time to time? Bad weather conditions affect our sturdy little vessel. High winds and rain, along with cold and hot temperatures seriously call into question the reliability of the boat to keep out water. From time to time, a big wave (rainstorm) causes water to leak into the rowboat. Consequently, the rowboat slows down and its power is weakened. If a tornado or hurricane passes in the path of the rowboat, you can

INTRODUCTION

be slowed to a near stop. This is in effect, what happens to individuals when the relationships they are in go sour. Their vitality and vigor for life becomes diminished when negative and toxic emotions adversely affect them. Recall how it feels when you lose a close friend who you bonded with for several years, or any other human tragedy. Well, that devastation that you felt is similar to what has happened to someone aboard this fictionalized boat.

As Emotional Core Therapy explains, it is the entering and leaving of relationships that can cause tension and stress in our lives. Examine the list below of commonly occurring stressful events in life that can cause debilitating feelings of fear and loss.

1. Death of a family member including grandparents/parents/sibling/etc
2. Divorce or separation of parents
3. Major health problem such as cancer, diabetes, etc
4. Being fired or reprimanded at work
5. Problems or disputes with relatives or close friends
6. Pregnancy
7. Being bullied at school
8. Failing grades at school
9. Catching your boyfriend or girlfriend cheating
10. Parents having to relocate for their job
11. Spilt or breakup with boyfriend/girlfriend
12. Changing your high school or college plans
13. Major weather disaster such as hurricane or tornado

14. Loss of important leisure or sports activity due to injury
15. Being harassed at school
16. Loss of home due to parents' economic hardship
17. Long standing disagreements with parent or other family member
18. Getting in trouble with the law
19. Change in health of close friend or family member
20. Close friends move out of state/out of town

Any one of the above stressful events would cause any human being to suffer. The real difference is that emotionally healthy people, including those practicing ECT, appropriately process their feelings.

The most common state of a person that successfully has learned ECT is one of tranquility and a balanced equilibrium. Meditation helps a great deal in this regard. It is one of the highest forms of self-care or self-love, and is critical to healthy development. As a culture, we need to do more to support the individual's need to take care of oneself/love oneself. This is especially important for teens, because in most cases nobody has ever taught them how to bring themselves to a reflective / meditative state. The good news is, there are literally hundreds of ways to meditate – and the benefits are amazing!

When one is very comfortable with this loving/meditative lifestyle they can truly defend themselves from society's pressures which are bombarding them day in and day out. How can this be achieved? Over time, your body can become

INTRODUCTION

readily able to identify foreign feelings such as joy, grief, fear, and relief. As a therapist I often tell my clients to embrace toxic feelings of fear and grief! Why? They (debilitating feelings) are telling you that something is wrong. While these feelings affect all of us, the fact of the matter is, joy, grief, fear, or relief does not dominate an emotionally healthy person. These four authentic feelings are just temporary states that affect the person from time to time. Let's face it, a perfectly smooth running rowboat does not exist. It is not realistic. What is realistic is that one can expect some minor water coming in from time to time. In rare instances, a rushing torrent of flooding water threatens to sink the rowboat – a perfect analogy for when we need to seek out professional help. Every community has some really awesome therapists, social workers, doctors, etc. who have dedicated their lives to helping people just like you. If you need them, don't ever hesitate to seek them out. After all, that is what they are there for.

An emotionally healthy person practicing ECT is committed to a life of having peace and comfort in their day. Their mind is allowed to daydream and reflect. Reflection is key as it is a relaxed way the mind can roam and wander from thought to thought in an effortless manner. The bottom line is, there is just no substitute for taking time for yourself daily. It is a way of respecting your self to allow your self, the time to be rested and peaceful. Here is a list of 40 popular ways to relax:

1. Exercise before school, get the blood flowing
2. Practice yoga, Pilates, or chi gong

3. Reduce the amount of caffeine you drink (especially soda!)
4. Go for a run around the block when you have some free time at home
5. Practice deep breathing throughout the day
6. Get your daily chores out of the way now instead of worrying about them
7. Cut out the excess sugar in your diet (it causes stress)
8. Throw out stuff around your house / bedroom you really don't need or use
9. Do some gardening in the yard
10. Get some fresh air by taking a brisk nature walk
11. Breathe deeply
12. Do some deep muscle stretches
13. Practice sewing or needlework
14. Go somewhere where sunlight warms your face
15. Call some old friends and spend some time hanging out and catching up on things
16. Tidy your room and make your bed so it's clean when you go to sleep
17. Head down to the beach and walk in shallow water
18. Escape by reading a relaxing book
19. Take some allotted time to do nothing at all
20. Go to bed early
21. Drink some lemon tea or green tea
22. Take a day off from your after-school job (with the boss' permission of course!)
23. Go and see a comedy show

24. Get a neck or a foot massage
25. Go for a walk around the markets or somewhere with lots of natural produce
26. Ride a bike in nature
27. Read a book you enjoyed when you were a little kid
28. Get off the computer and relax your eyes
29. Listen to some classic rock
30. Play a sport such as pickup basketball or bowling with friends just for fun
31. Watch a movie or TV show
32. Say a reflective prayer over and over in a relaxed chant
33. Sing to yourself in a humming or relaxed manner
34. Journal, draw or paint your random thoughts
35. Watch your thoughts without engaging them
36. Go fishing or boating
37. Spend some time with your dog or other animal
38. Pick up a hobby you have neglected
39. Let your imagination wander with some vacation you'd love to take in the future
40. Go out to a favorite restaurant for dinner

OK, at this point, you may be saying, thanks for that great list, but really, why would someone possibly write another self-help book? After all, ECT sounds interesting, but there are many excellent psychology books out there that do a great job at highlighting specific psychology techniques. So why add yet another book?

First and foremost, people are still suffering emotional trauma day in and day out. Look at America's prison system. We have several million people incarcerated in our jails and prisons, with millions of others on probation or parole. On top of that, we have thousands of people in psychiatric hospitals. Moreover, we have millions of people who are in so much pain that they are either under a doctor's care, or are self medicating through illegal drugs or alcohol to numb the pain. It's a gigantic national problem.

Much of this pain can be avoided with proper care of one's emotional health. That is why I think it is so important for people to learn the techniques of Emotional Core Therapy, especially at a young age, which is the primary purpose of this book. It is a way to take care of yourself in a preventive manner. Think about all of the other self-care techniques that you employ every day. Taking a shower and brushing your teeth for example. Both of these daily habits help keep disease away. ECT is also a daily habit, that when used correctly can help maintain one's health. Even better, it is so simple that normal everyday people can practice the technique. No special training required!

Is ECT the only route to mental health? Not at all. As we said, there are lots of other effective therapies and plenty of good self-help books out there. But ECT does tackle, head on, the fact that relationships, toxic or harmful, are a part of life for everyone. They are unavoidable. The only thing you

INTRODUCTION

can really do is to educate yourself on what is a healthy relationship. A healthy relationship can only begin if one is emotionally healthy. A healthy or stable person, as seen through the lens of ECT is a person who has full awareness of the four authentic feelings, joy, grief, fear, and relief. Furthermore, a healthy person knows how to live a relaxed and meditative lifestyle.

A healthy relationship is built on mutual respect. The communication style is one of openness and honesty. Lying and stealing are not part of a healthy relationship. Being able to trust and share one's authentic feelings is paramount to a healthy relationship. One can only do this if the relationship allows for a caring atmosphere to exist where all feelings are welcomed and understood. This means that one has to be able to share feelings of fear and loss as well as joy and relief.

One of the most important benefits of Emotional Core Therapy is that you begin to examine why particular relationships cause you debilitating feelings. This enables you to learn from your relationships and make better "relationship choices" next time. You begin to empower yourself by identifying and participating in healthy relationships, which in turn leads to more hope for the future.

This book about Emotional Core Therapy is meant as a teaching tool. That is why we use the approach of story telling – it is a great way to teach as you can learn through others' experience in a joyful, non-threatening manner.

The alternative, simply ignoring our emotional needs or seeking relief in unhealthy ways, can prove disastrous. Oftentimes people begin to learn inappropriate self-soothing techniques and bad habits in their teens. My hope is that by writing in a short, story telling, easy to read style, you will avoid these and start to learn to process your feelings in a safe and healthy manner.

Is ECT guaranteed to solve our problems, and how long does it take? First of all, nobody can guarantee anything in this life. All we can say regarding ECT is that it has proven to be a very effective and successful approach. But time and will (motivation) are needed for this approach to fully work. Why? Mature relationships – friends, school, boyfriend / girlfriend, etc. – frequently require the needs of others to be met. Even our own needs often have to be met in relationships. Whether it's emotional, financial, spiritual, or physical, humans are often required or asked to meet the needs of others in relationships. A key point of ECT is the concept of working to meet the needs of one's self or others in relationships.

As we begin to discuss the benefits of ECT we need to point out that some people may have to work longer and harder to reap these benefits. There are individuals who have impairments with one or more of their five senses (seeing, touching, smelling, tasting, and hearing). These impairments can cause their feelings of joy, grief, fear, and relief to be adversely affected. For example, a visually impaired person may not

INTRODUCTION

receive the same response watching a movie at the theatre as a non-visually impaired person. Also, there are individuals who have suffered severe early childhood trauma that is permanent in nature. For example, a child suffering from fetal alcohol syndrome may have some sensory problems that effect the ability to sense and feel. It is not that some of the benefits of Emotional Core Therapy will not be utilized, but the desired outcome of learning ECT may be harder than usual.

What other situations would arise that would cause ECT to not be successful? This book outlines situations and exceptions to where ECT may not have success. Like all treatment approaches people have to be comfortable with the process. Having the book told in a "simple storytelling fashion" is a means that has been successful with other psychological techniques, and I hope and trust that you will find it very helpful here as well.

So if you're ready to finally love yourself to the core, to love yourself enough to care for yourself emotionally in ways that will improve your life forever, keep reading. You're in for a journey that will transform the quality of your being.

5 Step ECT Flow Chart

Relationships;
self, other people, places, things

⇩

Four Authentic Feelings;
joy, grief, fear, relief

⇩

Uncomfortable Symptoms;
muscle tightness, fatigue, etc.

⇩

Releasing Process;
learn to discharge toxic feelings

⇩

Balancing Your Equilibrium;
practice various daily meditative techniques

CHAPTER ONE
How ECT Works

One of the most incredible things about being human is how many emotions we have. Emotions, also called "feelings," have an effect on everything you do every single day. Imagine if you had better control over your emotions – if you understood them and knew how to deal with them more effectively. Think that would improve things in your life? Of course it would, which is why looking at the "big picture" is such a good place to start. First of all, how many emotions are there? It's hard to pin an exact number to it, but there are hundreds of them at the very least. Here is just a partial list of some of the many ways that we express ourselves:

1. Loving
2. Wonderful
3. Joyous
4. Happy
5. Peaceful
6. Satisfied

7. Ecstatic
8. Content
9. Serene
10. Pleased
11. Elated
12. Excited
13. Overjoyed
14. Glad
15. Festive
16. Thrilled
17. Enthusiastic
18. Eager
19. Cheerful
20. Optimistic
21. Anxious
22. Fearful
23. Tormented
24. Nervous
25. Pessimistic
26. Depressed
27. Helpless
28. Disappointed
29. Upset
30. Bitter
31. Frustrated
32. Inflamed
33. Incensed
34. Tense

35. Irritated
36. Skeptical
37. Unsure
38. Rejected
39. Offended
40. Heartbroken

I'm sure you could add a lot more of your own, but you get the point. People are feeling emotions all the time and they can spell the difference between the best day you've ever had and the absolute worst. Not to mention everything in between. It sounds complicated, but with Emotional Core Therapy these hundreds of different feelings can all be broken down, or categorized into one of *four authentic feelings*. These are **joy, grief, fear, and relief.** Remember these! They are the key. Once you've learned how to identify them, so many things that once left you scratching your head will now seem crystal clear.

It's also important to understand the role that stress plays in your life. Teenagers live with a huge amount of stress on a daily basis. Take a minute to think about all of the many things in your everyday life that cause you stress. Sometimes just thinking about all of that stress is stressful! Unfortunately, there is no magic formula for completely eliminating stress from your life. That's impossible. Each new day brings with it the possibility of stressful situations. Consider, for example, all of the stress that is involved in competitive sports (whether as a spectator or a participant). Athletics involve experiencing all four of the "four authentic feelings." Again, these are joy, grief, fear and relief. Watch or play just about any sport and it won't take long before you recognize one or (more likely) all four of these feelings popping up. As a therapist, my main focus in counseling athletes and all of my other clients is to have them understand these four authentic feelings.

In simple terms all four true or authentic feelings evolve from entering and leaving relationships. OK, what the heck does that mean? Don't get confused by the word "relationships." Used in the context of ECT, it doesn't necessarily have anything to do with "romantic" relationships (which is probably what you assumed). Think of it instead more in terms of entering or leaving different situations, as you will see from some of the examples below.

Let's take a look at the following diagram.

Flow Chart of Four Primary Feelings

CHAPTER ONE

As you can see from this diagram, when you go towards something you like there is "Joy". What is Joy? In simple terms, it is a pleasurable state of arousal. If you ask someone, "what makes you joyful?" they will probably describe a relationship they are happy about entering into. An example would be seeing your favorite sports team win a close game. Another example would be hugging a loved one or someone you admire. Do you now see what I mean by "entering into a relationship"?

On the other hand, when you leave a relationship that you enjoyed, the result is grief. For example, leaving your warm, cozy house on a rainy day. Or it might be saying good-bye to your dog when you go off to school in the morning.

This diagram also shows what happens when you enter a relationship that you dislike. A relationship that you dislike will provoke feelings of fear. Imagine climbing inside a cage with a hungry lion. Entering into that relationship would no doubt make you experience fear! The same goes for jumping into the ocean if you don't know how to swim.

But what happens when you leave a situation that you dislike? There is relief. You escape out of the cage and slam the door on that hungry lion that wanted you for a snack. Or you finally reach the shore – and kiss the dry ground – after almost drowning in the ocean. These are great examples of relief!

This flowchart of four authentic feelings is critical to understanding Emotional Core Therapy. Feel free to go ahead and test it for yourself. All you have to do is substitute several of your own relationship experiences for those that we have listed here. Try a bunch for each authentic feeling and you will see exactly how these feelings are influencing throughout the day.

As the ECT Flowchart below highlights, it is relationships that spark the four authentic feelings in us. Specifically, relationships with our selves or others usually involve needs being met. For the sake of simplicity, I organize needs into four categories. Emotional, financial, spiritual, and physical. The benefit of ECT is that it helps you to easily identify your feelings, which gives you incredible control over your own life, as you learn how to release these feelings in an appropriate way. It helps get you into a calm, meditative frame of mind that is free from stress.

CHAPTER ONE

5 Step ECT Flow Chart

| Relationships;
self, other people, places, things |

⇩

| Four Authentic Feelings;
joy, grief, fear, relief |

⇩

| Uncomfortable Symptoms;
muscle tightness, fatigue, etc. |

⇩

| Releasing Process;
learn to discharge toxic feelings |

⇩

| Balancing Your Equilibrium;
practice various daily meditative techniques |

After studying the ECT flowchart several times, I want you to envision a particularly traumatic event in your life. Did your experience resemble the sequence highlighted in the five step

23

ECT flowchart? If so, in what way? If not, do not worry. We have the entire book to help you learn the ECT process.

When you enter a relationship that you like there is joy (remember, this is not limited to relationships with other people, as it could be many things; think of eating your favorite ice cream). When you leave something that you like there is grief (saying good-bye to someone you love – or finishing off the ice cream). When you go towards something you dislike there is fear. Imagine walking near a snake pit. When you leave a fearful event, there is relief (running away from that snake pit as fast as you can should do the trick).

Have you ever played sports? Well, then you know, the tougher your opponent, the tougher the test is for you emotionally. Grief (otherwise known as loss) and fear (otherwise known as anxiety) are the two most debilitating feelings that all athletes face when they play. In some cases, every game that you play is filled with these unwanted feelings. For example, if you're a football player you maybe start feeling anxiety every Friday afternoon during the fall, simply because you know that you will be playing in a game later that night. The point is, whatever your sport, at every level you need to get a handle on your emotions before game time rolls around – or face the consequences.

Hopefully, this is all starting to make sense to you. Yet, you very well might be asking, "Well, that's great for sports… but what about everything else in life?" My answer: there is no area of life where ECT will not be able to help you. We all need to find healthy ways to process our emotions every single

CHAPTER ONE

day, wherever we are and whatever we are doing. It doesn't matter how old you are, your financial circumstances, your love life or anything else. Your emotions are always there. They are an essential part of who you are. It makes no sense to try to bury them or to ignore them. Even if you could, you wouldn't want to, when you think about how lame and boring it would be to live in a world without feelings. Some people try, through drugs, alcohol and countless other means – but they inevitably end up harming themselves and lots of other people in the process. That's because they never learned a healthier way to cope with "toxic" feelings. Think of ECT as a lifestyle choice that will improve your mental health.

Like any lifestyle change, what you learn through ECT will not take root overnight, but over the course of months or years. It has to become a part of your everyday life, and in the process it will help your life to be more centered. How? By starting with the reality that grief and fear are an inevitable for all of us. You already know that's true, so why not equip yourself for something so common in life? Learning ECT is easier than it looks.

The real work of this book is to understand five major concepts (understanding relationships, authentic feelings, mind and body distress, releasing feelings, and dutiful meditation). Three other concepts (various needs being met, the role of our five senses, and the central nervous system being affected) occur quite quickly and without much thinking, but we will still examine them more closely in the final chapter.

Part of the overall ECT process we do instinctively anyway! For example, we enter and leave relationships all day long. So this is really not all that difficult for us to understand and follow. If you allow yourself the time to learn ECT, and are willing to commit the process to memory, you will very soon begin to see the results. Emotional Core Therapy is learning a process that will increase your enthusiasm and appreciation for life.

In order for ECT to be of real value, you need to be able to commit it to your long-term memory, which only happens through repetitious work.

How Memory Works

| Short Term Memory | • Input
• Thought | Short Term Memory | • Input
• Thought | Long Term Memory | Learned Behavior |

CHAPTER ONE

The goal is to never forget the process of how emotions work. We spend a year in high school learning Algebra, which many of us forget a few years later. That's OK if we go on to careers that never require Algebra. But we will always have emotions! So why not learn a process of emotional healing that will serve us our entire lives no matter where we live or what we do?

All of us humans know our dates of birth, our race, ethnicity, religion, etc. Why? We know these facts about ourselves because we learned them over and over again when were young. It takes time and energy to learn these important pieces of information about our life. In other words, practice, practice, practice. This information is useful and necessary as it serves to ground and center us as human beings.

Another way to understand how memory works is to think about Driver's Ed. Maybe you just got your driver's license, or will be doing so soon. How do you go about achieving this very important goal? When learning how to drive a car, you need to master certain things, and memory and repetition play a big role. Once you finally get that license, driving your own car opens up the world for you and you no longer feel restricted like you once did. The same goes for ECT.

Emotional Core Therapy is also an approach that will allow you to be centered in life. As ECT explains, grief and fear are an inevitable part of life. In any given year it is likely that one in five people will experience something that is emotionally devastating to them. Why not equip yourself for something so common in life? You will find an ECT Flowchart at the beginning of the book and at the end of each chapter as a reference point. This allows you to gauge how much you have learned about ECT after reading a chapter. A checkpoint of key ECT issues let's you focus on key concepts at a leisurely pace.

Let's now examine how the four authentic feelings are processed. It is our senses – seeing, touching, smelling, tasting, and hearing – that process of all of our feelings. As a therapist, over the years I have found that focusing on the release of authentic feelings has been helpful for clients' growth and development. Imagine that you are caught outside in a violent thunderstorm. If you are like most people you would get overwhelmed by emotions and lunge for the nearest umbrella. ECT, when practiced effectively, can downgrade a severe thunderstorm to just some minor drizzle. Emotional Core Therapy is effective because it filters out ambiguous words and negative thoughts by emphasizing and understanding the four true and authentic feelings.

It all begins with learning to continually monitor the four feelings. This approach offers hope even for those who have suffered the worst possible cases of trauma and abuse. Traumatic and stressful events, as most everybody unfortunately knows, come in a wide variety of shapes and sizes. The good news is that ECT is a helpful treatment option because it empowers you to assess your problems in a simple, yet effective manner.

CHAPTER ONE

The goal of Emotional Core Therapy is to get clients to be as peaceful and emotionally centered as a healthy two-year old. The definition of having a peaceful, relaxing, and meditative state is to feel non-threatened, or effected, by the four authentic feelings. Envision an infant in a crib, smiling and relaxed. Just as an infant can sit in a crib in a blissful state, a teen or an adult can also achieve a calm and relaxed state of being. As you read this book you will learn techniques to achieve meditation throughout the day. Meditation, a calm state of being, is essential for the successful use of Emotional Core Therapy, and makes it much easier to identify the four authentic feelings. It is crucial for people to learn at a young age how to love themselves. Only when you truly love yourself can you begin to control your destiny as a human being. ECT teaches us how to love ourselves by properly identifying what it means to be an "Emotional" human being.

To illustrate why this is so important, consider for a moment a high school senior named Charlie who is getting ready to take his ACT test. He is taking his ACT prep class along with Advanced Placement Chemistry and Honors English. Charlie is overwhelmed (ECT defines this as too much fear or excessive fear). He is also exhausted and has had trouble sleeping. It's clear that he needs to regain himself – but how? We view any type of relaxation or meditative state that allows you to reflect and daydream as a way to self-care or love oneself. Charlie was able to daydream by shooting baskets in his driveway. Whenever he had his basketball in his hands it served as a way for Charlie to rejuvenate his body and release the stress that comes with schoolwork. Of course, shooting baskets or hoops will not work for everyone. Another boy may like drawing or sketching, while a different kid may like hanging out by the pool. The key point to remember is to keep this reflective state throughout the day so that you can identify and release the four authentic feelings of joy, grief, fear and relief.

Many people suffering from grief or fear (which, as we said, is also known as anxiety) come to my office in a sad state of affairs with little hope of feeling better. Emotional Core Therapy teaches techniques to help yourself learn how to process emotions properly, and in ways that are healthy rather than destructive. Remember that *the four authentic feelings ultimately all stem from either entering or leaving relationships.* Take, for example, a boy and a girl who are having a strained relationship. The real problem is that they both have to grow and learn about each other. With ECT, we pay attention to how each feels in the relationship. The girlfriend (Ashley) in this scenario tells the therapist, "I get scared when Brandon comes over to do homework and hang out with me some afternoons. I know that he works hard at school during the day. He's taking the SAT soon and I know it's been making him tense. Still, I cringe when he comes over because he's so stressed out that any little thing that I might say wrong can set him off and start a big argument."

With ECT, we focus on the meaning of her feelings. In this case, both words she uses, "scared" and "cringe" are different vocabulary names for the authentic feeling, "Fear".

CHAPTER ONE

What Ashley is saying is that this relationship she has entered into brings fear into her life from time to time. She is not saying that they have a terrible relationship. She just wants to work towards a better resolution in this particular situation.

No one deserves to live life with unwanted and toxic feelings. Moreover, holding back (or holding in) your feelings can be very harmful in the long term. ECT utilizes a wide variety of commonly known techniques to release feelings. One of the most popular is to "verbalize" one's feelings. By talking out your fears with a compassionate therapist, toxic feelings such as fear (otherwise known as anxiety) are released. This is called catharsis. That's a big word, but basically it simply means a cleansing of the soul. With ECT, we are vigilant about cleansing our soul. Just like you learned to brush your teeth and wash your hands as a daily habit when you were a little kid, your soul also needs this type of positive treatment.

There are other ways that Ashley can learn to cleanse her soul. She can journal, listen to music, exercise, meditate, etc. Throughout the book you will find examples of releasing techniques. If for example Ashley had come in with lots of complaints of fear/anxiety because she is afraid to confront her boyfriend for not listening to her, I may focus on her learning to be more assertive with her needs. In this example, the first step is identifying the fear.

This is similar to a young man on the high school basketball team who says that he has a panic attack every time he has to go to the line for a free throw. He has excess fear, which adversely affects his concentration. This leads to his shot being messed up of course, because he needs to be free of tension and smooth to be effective. When an athlete in any sport lets his feelings have a negative effect on his performance it is called "choking". In other words, his nerves get in his way. The smart solution is to let a coach and perhaps a therapist help him through his emotional problem. Both of them will be supportive, caring, and allow an environment for the student athlete to take risks, and to make changes if necessary. Do you see how this is similar to a girl suffering fear from her boyfriend? That's precisely why, when I use Emotional Core Therapy I encourage clients to take risks and make changes if they are suffering debilitating feelings of fear and loss.

Another example might involve a teenage girl who has to take care of her two young brothers after school every day. She tells her therapist, "I just feel so overwhelmed by them, and I hate that I sometimes yell or get angry at them." Clearly, she chose her words carefully. She used the word "overwhelmed" because the reality is that she has too much fear! She's fearful (worried, concerned…feel free to add your own) that she will "fail" to fully or adequately complete all of the many tasks and responsibilities expected of her by her parents. The solution, then, is that she needs to be organized and structured in such a way so that she can feel a sense of accomplishment for the important contribution that she is making for her busy family (both parents work outside the home all day).

CHAPTER ONE

We all get overwhelmed from time to time. The dictionary definition of "overwhelming" is overpowering in effect or strength. Let's consider what is really happening to this young lady in terms of the four authentic feelings. Without a doubt, she is moving towards someone or something she does not like. Let me be clear, I am not saying that he does not like her young brothers. In fact, part of her fear is that, because she loves them so much, she's desperately afraid of failing both them and her parents. She fears that she might not be up to the task, however, because it includes so many things that worry her. For example, she may love to ride bicycles with her brothers. But then the two boys invite their two friends, meaning that their older sister is now responsible for four kids. What then happens if they ride their bicycles near a busy street? The situation, she fears, could very easily spin out of control. What was once manageable and enjoyable, is now overwhelming.

Emotional Core Therapy will help this teenage girl by isolating the problem, assessing the cause, and providing appropriate relief. We see that additional fear creeps into her thinking about this new activity when more children are involved, and in a more dangerous situation. When you have too much fear, it's important to reduce it somehow, if possible. A beneficial approach may be to highlight the new tasks and responsibilities involved in the four children scenario. By focusing on how this girl feels (muscle tension, lack of sleep, headaches, etc.) we can get her to modify her activities with her children. In the future, once she learns the technique, she can utilize ECT in other fearful, stress-inducing situations. Examples might be when she feels too much fear at school, or in other relationships. The point is, once you learn the techniques for processing your four authentic feelings, you will be amazed at how much this knowledge makes fundamental differences (for the better) in your everyday life and in the "big issues" (family, health, relationships, finances, etc). When I speak of "big issues" I mean "life events". Emotional Core Therapy has the ability, when used correctly, to completely change your outlook on life for the better.

Remember earlier in this chapter we used the analogy of a thunderstorm versus drizzle to show how you can feel less overwhelmed when using ECT? The beauty of this is that we can use it with just about any of life's problematic events. With Emotional Core Therapy we funnel all of these life events into two categories: entering and leaving relationships. Emotional stress is caused by moving towards or away from a relationship you have with a person, place, or thing.

This represents a crucial step in ETC, because once you can categorize all of your life events into two categories instead of two hundred, or two thousand, you gain control over the stress. You empower yourself by recognizing that the event is separate from you. You gain confidence that this event is something you chose in your life, and (if you want to) you can leave it, by properly processing your feelings.

CHAPTER ONE

Let's look at a particularly stressful event in this manner. A young man has just accepted a part time job offer at a local store. Once he starts his new position, however, he discovers that his boss is a lunatic. He knows that he cannot work there for very long without undue psychological stress. By utilizing Emotional Core Therapy, he recognizes that he has entered into a new relationship with someone. In this case, a new boss. Although he has a great deal of fear related to his current life predicament, he nevertheless feels confident deep down. Why? The boy recognizes that he is not the problem. Yes, he will have to grieve the loss of quitting and getting a new job. Yet, he knows deep down that these feelings will pass. He recognizes that he can process these feelings appropriately through the various techniques that he has learned in his counseling. Utilizing ECT can allow for this very difficult life event to be manageable for this young man.

We are now ready to begin to explore the most commonly occurring emotional stresses in the life of teenagers just like you. In the upcoming chapters we will examine various scenarios which are common to teenagers. We will show how ECT can be effective in helping teens gain peace and confidence in their lives.

As you read the various scenarios unfolding before your eyes, you can finally begin to learn the benefits of Emotional Core Therapy. In my work as a therapist, the most common psychological issues I see are depression, anxiety/fear issues. Most of these stresses to our equilibrium occur when we are with family, friends, at work, school, or in a relationship with someone of the opposite sex. As you become more and more acclimated to the ECT process, you will begin the healthy journey back home to your self. Think of the movie, "The Wizard of Oz." The main character, Dorothy, relates to the "Good Witch of the North" at the end of the film, repeating over and over, "There is no place like home." This reassuring chant allows her to leave the fantasy world of Oz and return home to Kansas. This is the mantra that you need to learn to fully comprehend Emotional Core Therapy. Every person is lovable. Every person deserves peace. Every person can overcome their troubled emotional state.

Keep in mind that Emotional Core Therapy works if you allow the process to work. If you are willing to make a genuine effort to grow and develop as a human being, what you read in the following pages will be transformational in your life. Over time, ECT will empower you by giving you the confidence that you can overcome any of the major traumatic events in life. There is simply no cure for the emotional trauma that life throws at us from time to time. It is how we respond to these hurtful events that defines us as human beings. ECT will teach you how to strengthen your mind and lift up your spirit.

5 Step ECT Flow Chart

| Relationships; self, other people, places, things |

⇩

| Four Authentic Feelings; joy, grief, fear, relief |

⇩

| Uncomfortable Symptoms; muscle tightness, fatigue, etc. |

⇩

| Releasing Process; learn to discharge toxic feelings |

⇩

| Balancing Your Equilibrium; practice various daily meditative techniques |

List Five Alternative Words Used To Describe The Feeling Of "Joy"

A) GLAD

B) HAPPY

1.
2.
3.
4.
5.

Notes:

CHAPTER ONE

List Five Alternative Words To Describe The Feeling Of "Grief"

A) DEPRESSED

B) SAD

1.
2.
3.
4.
5.

Notes:

List Five Alternative Words To Describe The Feeling Of "Fear"

A) ANXIETY

B) DREAD

1.
2.
3.
4.
5.

Notes:

CHAPTER ONE

List Five Alternative Words Used To Describe The Feeling "Relief"

A) RELAXED

B) REPRIEVE

1.
2.
3.
4.
5.

Notes:

List Five Stressful Relationships (People, Places, Or Things) In Your Life

A) ATTENDING A NEW SCHOOL

B) FRIEND GETTING SICK OR ILL

1.
2.
3.
4.
5.

Notes:

CHAPTER ONE

List Five Ways You Can Relax In A Meditative State

A) SWIMMING

B) LISTENING TO MUSIC

1.
2.
3.
4.
5.

Notes:

CHAPTER TWO
Using ECT to Treat Depression

It's a fact, at some time or another, all of us feel depressed. It's just a part of life. There are all kinds of reasons for it, and not all depression is created equal. Sometimes we're just feeling a little bit down, other times the depression can be severe. But the good news is, Emotional Core Therapy offers realistic, creative solutions for every form of depression.

Consider what might be a "worst case" kind of depression scenario. We all remember the catastrophic tsunami in Japan, and all of the misery that it brought to so many people. Imagine being a teenager in a hard hit area of Japan. When the tsunami swept over your town, many of your family and friends were killed and your community was devastated. How bleak is that? Now if ever there were cause for depression, this would be it! What could anybody do to console you? Would this awful tragedy at such a young age leave you trapped in a deep depression for the rest of your life? How could you possibly recover?

OK, this may be a very extreme example, but I bring it up for an important reason. The truth is, every month and every year people do survive and recover from tragedies such as this throughout the world. They even overcome these seemingly insurmountable troubles without the benefit of ECT or any other therapy for that matter. How do they do it? All it really takes is time and will for things to get better if one appropriately allows the normal occurrence of processing feelings to take place. With ECT, people are taught that all of us have the power to overcome any loss or devastation that life may throw at us.

Time and therapy are an incredibly powerful combination. Of course, it requires trust on the part of the client, and both client and therapist must view themselves as partners in the therapy process. This in turn gives power to the client. How better to give power to the client than have the client become their own therapist?

There is, however, one big obstacle that too often gets in the way – before the process can even begin. It is very common for people to spend lots of energy running away from debilitating feelings of fear and grief. Teenagers do this every bit as much as adults – but in both cases they are running in the exact opposite direction. In ECT, the goal is not to avoid our feelings, but to learn from them. For example, a very talented teenager twists her ankle doing a back flip in gymnastics practice. She is so traumatized by the pain that she is shaken to the core with fear and decides to quit the gymnastics team.

Think how much better off this girl would be if she analyzed her feelings rather than attempting to bury them. Instead of hanging up her shoes and ending her career, she could ask her coach, "How did I land improperly? What caused the injury? What can I do to prevent it from happening again?" If she had learned Emotional Core Therapy, she would have understood how to respect her authentic feelings of fear, and then release it by discovering how to improve her technique, rather than quitting the sport.

How can she do this (respect her authentic feelings)? By learning how to monitor her own body and the signals that it is constantly providing to her. This is one of the keys to successfully using ECT, and it works for all kinds of situations in life. The releasing of feelings can involve any loss in life, or any fearful event. Since we are all unique, none of us will release our feelings in the exact same way. It's a bit of a discovery process. For example, there was a fifteen-year old boy named Justin who was having difficulty with some of his classes. Nothing seemed to help, until one day some new neighbors moved in next door. They had a boy the same age and the two soon became friends. It turned out that this kid had some of the same problems in school as Justin. They would have long conversations, and soon things began to improve for Justin. Why? The reason is because they shared something in common and just talking with this new friend helped Justin to release his feelings. The point is, releasing feelings is a very natural process, and often takes place in unexpected places and usually unintentionally. It does not by any means always have to take place in a therapist's office.

Another example could involve a young, shy 17-year old male. He falls head over heels for a girl at his high school. Sadly, after three months of intense dating, she abruptly breaks up with him. Emotionally devastated, he withdraws into a shell and stops dating altogether. Now ask yourself, would it haven been much more emotionally healthy for this young man to instead honor his pain of grief/loss? I believe yes! Rather than stop dating, he needs to accept the experience and view it as part of a learning process. Easy? No, not by a long shot. It takes time (often months and even years) to understand one's feelings, which is why it is a continual learning process to learn ECT. But the benefits are real and often life-changing!

As these examples illustrate, we can learn a lot by examining a combination of various real life and hypothetical scenarios of people just like you struggling with the stresses of life, which is precisely the approach of the rest of this book. The goal is to help teens learn how to cope effectively with debilitating feelings. One of the primary purposes of this book is to demonstrate several psychological techniques in a fun and relaxed manner. It is always comforting and helpful to know that others have gone through, and continue to experience, the very same kinds of situations that you do.

At its core, ECT involves externalizing one's feelings rather than internalizing them. There is a time and a place

CHAPTER TWO

for releasing feelings, and common sense must be used. What we are trying to do is to get our feelings outside of us, and this is a process that takes time, like learning to ride a bike or to swim. For example, imagine if you found out that one of your friends, jealous of your athletic abilities, told your coach a big lie about you that got you kicked off the basketball team. Do you think that you would just bounce back from something like that overnight? Of course not! The feelings of anger and loss would be all too genuine, and properly releasing them would not come quickly. On the other hand, however, it would be quite regrettable to put this off too long, which would be very unhealthy for both your mind and body. Toxic beliefs, if internalized, can cause unnecessary stress and damage to the body. This in turn leads to body function problems such as muscle tightness, hand sweating and trembling. Don't underestimate the seriousness of this. A person who is under stress all of the time is risking damage to their organs, which is of course extremely hazardous.

Imagine the situation of a junior in high school named Megan. She comes to therapy because she finds that she is in a depressed state. Megan is suffering from major states of depression such as agitation, bad mood, no joy, oversleeping, lack of energy, and feeling useless. Both of her parents work so many hours that they can't give her much attention, and she is an only child. To make things worse, Megan had caught her best friend sneaking around with her boyfriend behind her back. At first she forgave him – but then he did the same thing with another girl. This time their break-up was permanent.

When Megan first begins therapy her level of depression is about an eight or nine (on a scale of one to ten). If she was already under a psychiatric doctor's care for depression, chances are good that the prescription medications she would be on might take the edge off her feelings, but they still would not lift her out of her funk. When Megan complains of being "unloved, unwanted, lonely, sad, tired," and crying a great deal, it will not be difficult for her therapist to assess her problem as too much grief or loss. Too much grief or loss is another name for depression. Megan is also suffering several bodily symptoms including lack of sleep, trouble eating and feeling fatigued.

Using Emotional Core Therapy, together she and her therapist would start to reframe some of her thinking. She will start to recognize that most of her thoughts are due to leaving a long-term relationship. Her overwhelming feelings of psychic pain will begin to lessen over time as she learns to isolate the problem. As she becomes more and more aware of the four authentic feelings, she is going to recognize that she has too much grief in her life. Over the course of eight to ten months, she will begin to release her feelings both in therapy and in her daily life.

Emotional Core Therapy will teach Megan that another way to combat her depression is by working to bring more joy into her life. For example, her therapist would probably urge her to make a list of twenty attributes that she likes about herself. As they discuss the list of twenty joyful characteristics, they will see if a main theme continues to pop up. For example, let's say Megan has a wonderful and truly loving relationship with her grandparents. They live across town but whenever she can she takes the bus and visits them, and they are always so happy to see her. Using this information, Megan's therapist would highlight how she was able to bring joy to her grandparents' life, and in turn to her own.

As part of using ECT, Megan would also start to do things that bring her joy herself. For example, power walking for exercise and stress reduction, along with making new friends who are much more respectful of her needs. This will help Megan to reduce her level of depression from a seven or eight level to a three to five level over the course of her therapy.

If Megan drops in for a visit to her therapist a few years later, in all probability she will look much better. She may well be a senior in college engaged to a great guy whom she truly loves. Emotional Core Therapy can't promise such results – nothing can – but it can definitely offer a teen like Megan hope that she might otherwise never have.

Prescription medications alone are unlikely to be as effective as ECT. They might numb Megan's pain but they would do little to change her underlying condition of a poor relationship. Her therapist would work with her to decrease her medication until eventually she doesn't need them at all. This will allow Megan the opportunity to reduce her self-described addiction to prescription drugs and begin to change her life for the better.

Many people try to self-medicate in a number of different ways, including teenagers. Some like to lose themselves in partying, while others choose to rebel against their parents. They are using these things as a way of trying to avoid loss or grief. What they fail to recognize, however, is that these feelings are a natural and normal part of life. When using Emotional Core Therapy to treat depression, you will learn the proper coping mechanisms for processing grief. The time varies from person to person and from one situation to another. The severity of the situation makes a big difference. Losing a five-dollar bill is not going to cause as much as grief as finding out that you have cancer. The real problem with drowning your pain away or numbing yourself is that it does not work. It only delays the inevitable: at some point you have to fully grieve the loss.

Emotional Core Therapy teaches us to calm the body by staying in a peaceful, meditative state throughout the day. By remaining this way for a prolonged period you can identify all fearful and toxic events in your life. This includes drugs or alcohol. A person that understands how a hot stove works would not touch it because they understand that it causes burns and pain. The same can be said for drugs and alcohol. Why would you use something that could cause legal and financial trouble? Why would you use something that could cause so much damage to your body or even kill you?

CHAPTER TWO

Do the research! Go on the Net and find out for yourself. The more information one has about illicit drugs or alcohol, the less likely they will be to use them. Would someone really want to use methamphetamine (also known as "speed"), for example, if they knew the harm that it could cause to their body, or heroin, if they fully understood that an overdose could kill them? As if that weren't bad enough, with illegal drugs nobody knows exactly what is in it, meaning it often includes toxic substances that can be deadly. You need to notify your medical doctor when you have any mental health problems, but especially problems with addictions, because medical doctors have a good understanding of these issues and how to address them.

Oftentimes young people seek out legal or illegal drugs, alcohol, or prescription drugs to numb the emotional pain of fear or grief. But rarely, if ever, does this work to treat the underlying issue. You have to change the relationship issue that is causing you emotional trauma to fix relationship problems. Let's look at a high school tennis player for an example. When he begins his serve, he twists his back a certain way every time, because of poor technique. Every day, he comes home and takes a pain reliever for his shoulder and back pain. The medication will not change his poor technique that is causing the problem in the first place. This young tennis player needs a coach to teach him a proper serve with less torque so he won't twist his back out every time. By changing his behavior (poor swing) the boy learns a proper swing and won't have to take medications continuously. Besides, medications, drugs, and alcohol, usually have side effects which can hurt your performance in tennis matches. Ever see a tennis player with a headache and a hangover play! Not a pretty sight!

Now let's look at a real life situation. A high school freshman girl enters her math class. She gets a grouchy old man, near retirement, as her teacher. The old man is mean to all the kids. He yells and gives detentions out all the time. It is a legal form of abuse. The young girl sees her high school counselor who in turn refers her to a psychiatrist who prescribes her medication to relax. What is wrong with this picture? Why not change the relationship that is causing this stress in the first place? Get a new teacher! Switch schools! Complain to the principal, etc. The point is, if the young girl can change her relationship with the teacher, she won't need to take medications or drugs for years and years. She can honor her authentic feelings of fear and work towards a result that will release those feelings. Better yet, when she is a senior, and she is assigned "a mean old hag" as a chemistry teacher, she will know how to assert herself. Not only that, but when her new boyfriend causes her fear by teasing her in front of her friends, she will know exactly what to do! Why? The techniques of ECT are easy to learn and can be transferred from situation to situation. They provide your life with a sense of power and vitality that you will never experience if you lose yourself in a haze of drugs and alcohol.

Consider a scenario of someone who decides to smoke pot every day to cope. What happens? She may get suspended.

Miss valuable school time. Get in trouble with the police. Hurt her chances for acceptance to a good college. Not to mention she will have to deal with the side effects of marijuana like fatigue and lack of energy. Probably not a smart way to try to cope.

ECT, by stark contrast, offers a genuine way to cope with problems, and it can also help with addictions (both kicking them and never developing them in the first place). Since addictive tendencies often begin during the teen years it's very important for you to learn how properly releasing your authentic feelings can help you to avoid all kinds of big problems down the road. Here is a list of some of the most common addictions (it does not include the abuse of narcotics, as it is a list of legal addictions, but the use of illegal drugs of course can lead to serious and even fatal addictions for lots of individuals, including young people).

10. Shopping

Compulsive shopping may sound funny, but it's very serious and can have disastrous consequences for your finances.

9. TV

It's hard to experience real life when you spend half the day plunked in front of the TV. Your teenage years are a great time to learn about the world – by actually experiencing it.

8. Video Games

The video game world is also not real life. Sure, it can be a fun way to spend time. But if you spend too much time on video games, they can indeed become quite addictive, keeping you away from more important and productive things.

7. Celebrity Gossip

Everybody likes to read stories about celebs, all the "who is dating who" stuff and the latest "dirt." But why get so caught up in the lives of celebrities? These aren't people that you know in your real life. Try to take only a passing interest in that stuff. Your time is too valuable for much more than that.

6. Fast Food

Yes, it's cheap and it tastes good. But you also know how unhealthy fast food is. If you get addicted to it as a teen, these cravings could become a habit for life – which is definitely something that you want to avoid.

5. Gambling

You may not be old enough to go to a casino yet, but lots of teenagers get caught up with gambling in a number of different ways, often involving sports. Bad idea. It almost always ends up losing money and can later develop into a very serious bad habit as an adult. Avoid it now rather than regret it later.

4. Pornography

OK, maybe it seems harmless at first. After all, you are at an age where thinking about sexual topics is completely normal and natural. So is being curious. But pornography is such an unhealthy way to explore one's sexuality. It objectifies human beings and conjures up misleading ideas about sex and love, and ultimately leads to addiction for many people. At that point, it is no longer harmless in any way.

3. Alcohol

First, if you are under 21 it is illegal for you to drink alcohol anywhere in the United States. Moreover, once a person starts drinking, it can be extremely difficult to stop and not get sucked in by this powerful addiction. Think of how many people are killed and maimed by drunk drivers every year. Not to mention what alcohol does to your liver and your brain. The last thing you want is to become yet another statistic.

2. Cigarettes

In recent years, the government and society at large have been trying to warn people about the dangers of tobacco.

Like alcohol, once you start it can be incredibly hard to stop. Cigarettes contain nicotine, which is highly addictive. Spare yourself from an early grave and never pick up this bad habit in the first place.

1. Prescription Drugs

At different times in our lives, we all need to take prescription drugs for very legitimate reasons. For example, you may have been injured playing sports and your doctor prescribed painkillers. The problem with these drugs is people can easily become dependent on them. Don't think that it can't happen to you! Other people, both your age and older, thought the same thing but soon ended up with a serious addiction crisis in their life. Use extreme caution even with drugs that are prescribed to you – and never use a drug that is not prescribed to you. That could land you either in jail or in the morgue.

Getting back specifically to ECT's treatment of depression, it can be very creative in the ways that it supports patients. For example, young man I talked to remembered the words of Bruce Springsteen's hit, "Born in the USA," a song about the troubled life of a returning Vietnam War veteran. We talked about that song, and sometimes we even play songs in therapy as a tool. There is something comforting about the song's powerful music and defiant lyrics, which seem determined to overcome all of the hardship. It helps relieve some of the grief to talk about whatever it is that hurts us, and it's a great way to help release feelings.

CHAPTER TWO

One of the reasons that music is such an excellent technique to release feelings is the sheer magnitude of songs. It could be Hard Rock, Rap, Pop, Country, you name it some artist has recorded a song for nearly every possible type of relationship issue or problem. All four authentic feelings have hundreds, if not thousands of songs that people can relate to in every culture and virtually every personal situation.

Another tool might be to talk about movies. Consider "Titanic" for example. It's a story of young love cut tragically short by one of the most famous disasters of the twentieth century. When a viewer watches this type of film it is possible to evoke some hidden feelings of loss. This kind of reading of toxic feelings happens to most of us daily in some fashion when we maybe watch some of the soaps on TV or listen to a sad song on your Ipod. None of this is meant to be morbid. The point is, hiding from grief does not make it go away and it does not cure depression. To the contrary, identifying the feelings of loss, is the first step in coping with those feelings, and sometimes things like songs and movies can help us put our finger on the problem spot.

The one common factor in each of the examples we are discussing is that they are all about loss. But simply knowing that is not enough. We need to explore deeper, to get to the roots of what these relationships were truly about.

Another client, Austin, was dealing with a different set of circumstances. He did not have a great voice in his family, and consequently never really had anyone to confide in.

His father was a hard driving workaholic, so Austin worked hard too. He took a job washing dishes in the kitchen of a nursing home, spent a lot of night hours at work, and didn't have many friends (and the few he did seemed to always be out having fun while he was working). Worse yet for Austin, his family lived in a secluded subdivision that not have many young people living nearby. So his issue coming to therapy was isolation and despair, which are terms otherwise known as loss or grief.

Using the authentic nature of ECT, I was able to show Austin how his feelings of grief were connected to his lack of friends and support. In therapy, I was able to draw a small picture of how the four authentic feelings work and Austin was able to see that his powerful feelings of sadness were situational to his job, where he lived, and spending so much time away from friends. When Austin began counseling with my office he was near a nine on the one to ten point scale of sadness ratings. This was however a temporary state. We discussed Austin's early childhood where he was often very happy playing ice hockey with his friends. He was able to see his feelings of grief were tied to entering a new relationship (in a new job isolated from people his own age)

As part of our therapy, Austin made a list of ten things that would bring him joy. His top five wishes were better grades, a scholarship for college, a new car, a new girlfriend, and more time with his friends. Over the course of the next 14 months, Austin began to work towards those five dreams that would bring him joy. He was able to achieve two to three of his desired ways to bring joy into his life. His level of grief plummeted from an eight or nine to two to four as Austin began to feel more supported and loved in his life.

In therapy, he was honest about his feelings. He genuinely wanted to get better. One of the first big decisions he made was to ask his boss to cut back his hours working in the kitchen at the nursing home. His boss agreed, and Austin soon started spending more time with his friends on nights and weekends, sometimes just hanging out, other times playing hockey with them. This made him feel more connected not only to other kids his own age, but to life itself. You see, it was important for Austin to build a support network so that he would not feel so isolated.

Emotional Core Therapy uses various techniques to help people help themselves to get better. In this case, we helped Austin to recognize what he wanted out of life. He wanted a girlfriend, a new car, and some relaxation doing fun stuff with friends. At the time, he had none of these things, but he recognized that he could work for them and – most critically – he had the power to get them.

The ECT therapist is like a cheerleader: very supportive of the patient. They go at their own speed and of their own volition. It wasn't the therapist's role to tell Austin what to do. He, like every patient, has to work that out on his own. The therapist is there to support him, trying different things, to assist him in his journey to recovery.

The therapist helps the patient to not be fearful about obtaining what they want from life. Don't let anyone ever tell you that you are too young to know these things about yourself. After all, it is *your* life, and whatever your age, you are the only one who can live it. In ECT, we talk about basic feelings so if there is something that you are afraid of, we want to explore that. We teach people to be respectful of themselves and to acknowledge that they are indeed worthy of working everything out. No, it doesn't come overnight. For example, in Austin's situation he was able to achieve two of his goals, but not all of them – at least not initially. But what really matters is that he was able to bring joy into his life. That was missing when all of his focus was on his depression and he felt utterly powerless to do anything about it.

Next, let's take a look at a hypothetical case involving a girl named Rachel, a high school student who loves spending time with her friends every chance she gets. The time that she spends with them both during and after school are at the center of her social life. That is when she talks with her friends about anything and everything, and she truly relishes those special moments.

But then something quite unexpected happens. Her father gets a new job in another state and the family has to relocate. For Rachel it is devastating. Being uprooted like this it feels like her life was ruined. She keeps in touch with her friends by phone and text, but it just isn't the same. She really cares about those kids, and losing them is more than just a major bummer – it causes her tremendous grief.

Using ECT, a therapist would help show Rachel how to process that grief. Rachel's parents don't have the training to help her with this, and she therefore needs outside assistance. ECT would allow her to tell the stories of her pain and to process her feelings in ways that are healthy and promote mental healing. She could also identify and label her authentic feelings of grief in therapy. These kinds of ECT sessions would likely be filled with crying and feeling angry with her parents for moving so far away from the only home she had ever known. She can no longer spend hour upon hour with her friends going to the mall and doing gymnastics and other fun stuff together. This is something that she must come to accept. Rachel would learn that there is no magic cure or pill for grief. It is a necessary part of life. We can only learn from the pain and become better individuals in the future.

In Rachel's case, she needs to make new friends at her new school and new neighborhood. She probably does not want to be a "loner" just because she is the new girl. ECT would show her that all of the good qualities that made her friends back in her home state (who were still her friends, albeit at a long distance) like her in the first place, would appeal to kids in this new place as well.

Using and processing authentic feelings of joy and grief in therapy, ECT would show Rachel that she needs to build up a new support network of friends where she now lived. She would be able to learn from her debilitating feelings of sadness and have more hope for the future. Just as our aspiring gymnast in an earlier example was better off learning from her painful ankle injury, Rachel would in turn be better off for processing and identifying her four authentic feelings of joy, grief, fear, and relief. She needs to be determined to make better decisions about when and where to make friends.

Oftentimes clients like Rachel need a hug, tissue, and a non-judgmental atmosphere to release their foreign feelings of sadness. If Rachel is a visual learner, she and her therapist would be able to diagram her supportive relationships and identify and isolate her feelings of loss. Both the visual and verbal means of expression would allow Rachel to release her sadness over a period of a few months. The goal would be to help her work towards making new friends, without giving up her old friends, so that she could strike the proper balance in her life.

One option might be for Rachel to begin to take (acoustic) guitar lessons to regain her sense of calm and peace. By strumming soft songs, she would be able to begin her process of self-care and self-soothing. Of course, it is important to again reiterate that what works for one client as a form of relaxation may not work for another. Rachel's mind needs to be allowed to daydream and relax through an activity such as playing the guitar. Other people may find learning to play a musical instrument a chore and mentally taxing. The exact form of relaxation that you choose isn't what really matters.

CHAPTER TWO

It does matter, however, that you discover the best way for you as an individual to relax. This is an important step in Emotional Core Therapy, as it allows the mind a way to daydream and flow freely.

Another hypothetical case involves an aspiring teen writer named Abby who dreams of being famous writer like her father. She had attended writing seminars during her first two summers in high school, took AP literature and hired a tutor to help improve her grades even further. Abby had even quit the swim team so she could stay after school and write short stories for her school newspaper.

The summer before her senior year, Abby applies to four of the best writing colleges on the East Coast. She is crushed by disappointment when all four reject her application. During her senior year, Abby often finds herself crying uncontrollably. She has trouble sleeping and eating and can barely concentrate in class. Her grades go into a free fall and she starts getting into arguments with her boyfriend.

What is really happening to Abby? She is suffering from excessive grief. This scenario could happen to most anyone in high school. How do we help someone in Abby's situation using Emotional Core Therapy? With ECT we would focus on authentic feelings of joy grief, fear, and relief. We would spend a good amount of time helping Abby cathartically release those toxic feelings of loss/grief, and spend some time helping her find joy in her life. This would include making a list of 20 things that bring her joy. Abby and her therapist would set a goal of trying to initially obtain at least four or five of these. The list would likely include simple things such as a day at a spa, getting ice cream, going to the movies, a day at the beach, etc.

Using ECT, Abby would also learn some loving yourself meditative techniques like taking a Jacuzzi, walking the dog, and many others. We would educate Abby on the definition of loving yourself and teach her the five-step ECT process. Near the end of therapy we would introduce all eight steps.

Later on in Abby's life, once she has committed ECT to her long-term memory, she will be able to transfer what she has learned to other situations/relationships. When her boyfriend breaks up with her she will suffer grief. When her grandmother gets sick and passes on, Abby will grieve. The difference is as an adult, she will learn much quicker how to identify and process the four authentic feelings of joy, grief, fear and relief. This will greatly improve her quality of life, and make it much less likely that she will suffer from long bouts of severe depression.

One other case that demonstrates ECT's effectiveness in treating depression involved a young man named Ryan, an eighteen-year-old recent high school graduate. Ryan had a girlfriend that he loved and adored. He worked for the family business, and the idea had been that he was supposed to make a lot of money following in his father's footsteps. But his father whom he worked for was very demanding. Moreover, the young man worked outside inside an office building all day, which he didn't really like at all.

In ECT therapy, we let him talk out his feelings. He shared things about himself, such as that when he was in high school he was a very good athlete. He was able to recognize and identify the things in life that brought him joy. These included working closely with people; he actually preferred to be working outside, not inside. As a matter of fact, he found great satisfaction working with his hands, rather than sitting at a desk all day.

Ryan could not shake his depression until he changed several of his relationships that were causing him grief. He was sad that he had to work underneath a demanding and mean spirited father. Ryan was also sad that he had to work an isolated job as an office worker, which meant he had to work indoors all day even when it was sunny and beautiful outside.

When Ryan came to see me his level of sadness/depression was at an eight or nine! Fortunately for Ryan, he had the time and determination to alter his relationships that were causing him grief. Over the course of twelve months, he was able to quit his job and go to a vocational school where he started training for a job with a major utility company. Ryan came back to visit me a year after therapy ended to report that he had proudly earned employee of the month at his new, much happier job. His level of depression dropped from a nine to a one or two in just over a year.

Of course, no two people experience depression in the exact same way or for the exact same reasons. Therefore, we always need to treat people as individuals with unique problems and solutions that depend upon their own particular circumstances. However, Emotional Core Therapy offers solutions based on abilities that all of us innately possess. The therapy is successful because it works *with* your emotions rather than treating them as some kind of enemy or outsider. Depression and sadness, after all, are natural aspects of life, but the sooner and more precisely we understand what brings them about, the closer we are to moving on to a happier and more peaceful frame of mind.

CHAPTER TWO

5 Step ECT Flow Chart

| Relationships;
self, other people, places, things |

⇩

| Four Authentic Feelings;
joy, grief, fear, relief |

⇩

| Uncomfortable Symptoms;
muscle tightness, fatigue, etc. |

⇩

| Releasing Process;
learn to discharge toxic feelings |

⇩

| Balancing Your Equilibrium;
practice various daily meditative techniques |

List Five Relationships That You Have Exited That Have Brought You "Grief"

A) MOVING OUT OF STATE

B) FAILING A CLASS AT SCHOOL

1.
2.
3.
4.
5.

Notes:

CHAPTER TWO

List Five Ways You Can Release Feelings Of Grief

A) JOURNALING

B) SINGING

1.
2.
3.
4.
5.

SYMPTOMS OF DEPRESSION

CRYING SPELLS FOR NO APPARENT REASON

LOSS OF INTEREST OR PLEASURE IN NORMAL ACTIVITIES

CHANGES IN APPETITE

FATIGUE, TIREDNESS AND LOSS OF ENERGY

FEELINGS OF SADNESS OR UNHAPPINESS

IRRITABILITY OR FRUSTRATION, EVEN OVER SMALL MATTERS

INDECISIVENESS, DISTRACTIBILITY AND DECREASED CONCENTRATION

List Five Of Your Own Symptoms Of Depression

1.
2.
3.
4.
5.

Notes:

CHAPTER THREE
Using ECT to Treat Anxiety

This chapter on anxiety will build on what you have already learned about Emotional Core Therapy. We will again use a variety of mostly fictional situations to illustrate how ECT helps you to live a better life and to solve problems with as little fear as possible.

Before going any further, let's ask a very simple question: what exactly is this debilitating feeling of "fear"? The simplest definition is that it is really just another word for "anxiety." As we discussed in the beginning of this book, it is entering a relationship that you dislike that causes fear. A good example of someone entering a relationship they dislike would be a child or a teenager living in a country torn by warfare. You have seen video on TV of what conditions are like in places such as Iraq and Afghanistan. Close your eyes and try to imagine that you lived under those circumstances, never knowing when a bomb might go off or gunfire could suddenly erupt. Any normal human being (of any age) would be fearful or afraid. In other words, your "relationship" with the war would make you experience fear. All of the cases in this chapter, though not nearly as extreme as warfare, will examine characters entering relationships that they dislike. You will see how ECT can potentially help in each of these situations.

The first example that we use involves a nineteen-year old named Drew. He came to my office complaining of feeling scared about his life. He was nervous that he was not his usual self. He was terrified that he was not living up to being a man. He joined the military, but once he got to boot camp he had a difficult time fulfilling the rigorous requirements and ultimately dropped out. Drew became worried about his self-esteem, and he felt weak for not being able to successfully complete boot camp. The experience was very demanding on the young recruit. The drill instructor was mean spirited, hostile and angry all day long. Drew would wake up at the crack of dawn with the drill instructor yelling at him. He would then be ordered around all day and night by this very demanding guy. Drew was pushed to his limits both physically and mentally during his thirty-day ordeal that included shooting guns off, sleep-deprivation, hot sun, and severe weather conditions.

When we examine some of the feelings that Drew faced we see that he used words such as terrified, nervous and scared. The primary feeling was fear – especially of failing family and friends. Some of Drew's symptoms included a loss of attention, lack of sleep, lack of concentration and fatigue. These are all classic examples of someone who is suffering from fear and anxiety.

For Drew a full recovery would occur within a few months of the counseling. A supportive environment for him to release his feelings of fear would be crucial to his recovery. The focus of treatment would be releasing Drew's traumatic experience. I emphasize traumatic because each situation is different for each individual. For example, there were young men in Drew's boot camp class who were able to successfully graduate without any psychological stress. Some people perceive situations as more stressful than others. So we have to honor each person's fear and how it impacts them.

Part of Drew's success in counseling was that he was able to fully express all the harmful events that happened to him. Moreover, because of his time in the counseling office, he learned that it was okay to express what was on his mind. In fact, it was very important to his recovery. Even the most horrendous thoughts or feelings are allowed to be expressed, whether they are accurate or not. We sort those out. I gave Drew several examples to practice releasing feelings at home. He was able to choose from a variety of ways to release his feelings. That's what we do with all of our clients. We give them the option to choose what they want to do based on their own world experience and what they like to do.

Some of the ideas include writing, journaling, drawing, listening to music, exercising, jogging, meditation, yoga, or

Pilates to name a few. Drew began to feel comfortable in therapy because he chose to freely verbalize his feelings. He started to do more talking, too, which he wasn't used to doing at home, where his family didn't really support expressing his feelings. Once he got into therapy, Drew became more expressive and he started to like it.

Every client is different in how they choose to express themselves. The best way for a therapist to do ECT is to work from a client's perspective and worldview. For Drew, learning to verbalize his unwanted feelings was a huge emotional growth step. He realized over time that it was okay to talk about negative feelings and to show his vulnerabilities. Drew also began to realize the value of cathartically releasing his feelings. He learned how to self-monitor his body for changes in his physical state, and realized that he was getting better as he started to release his feelings. Consequently, his fear level went down.

To examine how ECT helped Drew recover in this situation let's go back to the diagram in Chapter One on authentic feelings. Our brain receives authentic feelings such as fear. Once our brain, which is part of our central nervous system, senses these feelings, the muscles in our body respond. This sequence of events is helpful for our survival as human beings. If you are having trouble understanding this concept think of a situation which has occurred to most of us at home, touching at hot stove. If you accidentally touch a hot stove and burn your finger, you are not likely to repeat this mistake again. Why? We sense the fear as a result of the negative consequence that the action has on our body, i.e., a burnt finger and the accompanying pain. As for Drew, in therapy he learned to monitor his body and to pay attention to his body's feelings. I tried to have Drew monitor his feelings away from the counseling office. By doing this, he was then able to see his debilitating feelings of fear slowly dissipate out of his body.

Another step in Drew's recovery was the use of meditation and relaxation in his life on a daily basis. Drew had nightmares for months prior to entering therapy so it was important for him to learn to have a quiet state of being as part of his daily life. Every person in therapy relaxes in a different way. One person may like sitting in a Jacuzzi, while someone else might like yoga or Pilates, and others might like to do relaxing activities like bowling or walking a dog. The key to relaxing is to have the mind be free of tension, to be able to daydream, to reflect and be able to stay calm. Rather than actually thinking and using your mind actively, we want the mind to freely flow and to reflect. This differs for each person because each person relaxes in a different way.

Another term for relaxation is self-soothing. Everybody self-soothes in different ways so we have to go to their point of view. When we talk about different techniques of relaxation, what's good for one person is not necessarily good for another. You might have a friend, for example, who finds it relaxing to hang out at the mall and can release her feelings that way. But if you're the type who hates crowds, this would not work for you, since you would find it stressful and it would actually make things worse.

So you have to really pay attention to what each person feels helps his or her mind to relax. We have to go back to their history of what they did when they were younger to relax, and we always give people the option of what they want to do to relax. When we examined Drew's history we found that he enjoyed sitting in his room listening to music. While listening to different artists express themselves and their feelings Drew slowly felt his tensions easing away. This process, however, takes time. Once Drew was able to see how authentic feelings operate, he began to release his feelings. His recovery started when he realized that he didn't have to enter boot camp anymore. That was a situation and a relationship that he had entered into but it was separate from himself and he realized that he would never have to go back to it again. That was an important step for him and a critical component of Emotional Core Therapy, realizing that all relationships either grow or weaken. He realized that his relationship with boot camp was in the past, that he was separate from that and he could now start to release that fear. By doing this, Drew was finally able to take back control over his life. Once he understood that he was over this experience he could start to release the pain of it.

All the experiences that Drew had gone through in boot camp were separate from himself. He entered into these relationships and he left them. In therapy, he was reminded that he had succeeded in other events. So why not this event?

Another key for Drew was releasing pain through nature. Things such as trees and water, open land and spaces help the mind to daydream and wander. Imagine yourself sitting under a shady tree on a warm summer day. You listen to the wind blowing and the birds chirping. Looking around you see the beautiful trees of various shapes and sizes, and up above in the sky the beautiful clouds slowly drift past like a soft batch of cotton candy. When you go to this peaceful place you are able to reflect and daydream, allowing your feelings and thoughts to freely wander in and out of your mind.

One question we need to ask is why would Drew not be able to release his feelings? With ECT we recognize that the body has a way of protecting itself from foreign or outside feelings. It is not normal and healthy to have debilitating feelings of fear and loss in our lives. If you don't believe what I'm saying, envision a two-year-old girl or boy in a crib. If a two-year-old child has suffered the psychological pain of being yelled at or scolded constantly what would happen? By the same token what would happen if this two-year-old was in his yard and a strange dog came up barking in his face? Quite naturally, the child would start crying to show fear. The child would show visible pain and look for comfort. What would be the remedy? Quite possibly it would be a loving hug from a mommy or daddy or to take the boy away from the dog or the yard where the fearful event had occurred. If bitten, maybe a Band-Aid to stop the bleeding or a visit to the doctor for a shot to make sure that there are no diseases of infections. Every normal and healthy parent would do all that they could to help the child in pain. Why? Because a child cannot do these things themselves, and a two-year-old child cannot lie and deceive themselves about how they feel. They cannot hide pain. They have to release it somehow.

It is a natural process to release emotional pain by crying and whining. They have no defense mechanisms to block the cognitive emotions. Every loving parent would do whatever they could to protect this two-year-old and quite naturally console their pain. Why? The parent loves the child. It is a very powerful relationship.

It is also very important for each one of us to learn how to truly love ourselves. In ECT terms, the definition of loving yourself is to allow yourself a peaceful, meditative, and reflective state of mind throughout the day. The four authentic feelings – joy, grief, fear, and relief – are just temporary states that are certain to change. That is why it is important to not let any of them dominate your emotional self/psyche for too long, if you can help it.

The decision is yours! If you commit to loving yourself (allowing for a peaceful, meditative state of mind) then it becomes much easier to identify and process the four authentic feelings day in and day out. Over time, you learn to release and externalize the feelings of joy, grief, fear, and relief on a daily basis. Learning to love yourself is an important part of

CHAPTER THREE

growing up, and will serve you well throughout your entire life.

This same power of love is what has to transpire for Drew to get better. He has to respect himself enough to cheer himself and allow himself to get better. It was not a short process for full recovery but so long as Drew had the support of people around him a full recovery was expected. You see, the human body has a natural way of protecting us from danger. The psychological turmoil of sustaining things like fear and loss is dangerous to the human body. Drew has to allow himself to be held, comforted, and supported to be protected, just like this two-year-old. He has to respect himself and his feelings enough to allow himself to heal from this pain.

We are now ready to examine some other scenarios where ECT can help people in your age group to overcome debilitating fear and anxiety. Let's say there is a sixteen-year old boy named Aiden. He had a very happy and ordinary life, up until a few years ago when his parents divorced. He lived with his mother and saw his dad sometimes, though not as often as he would have liked. Then his mom married a guy named Floyd, who seemed decent enough. But the problem was Floyd's son, Jackson, who was about the same age as Aiden. Whereas Aiden was a good kid who worked hard in school, Jackson was the exact opposite. He was basically a slacker, the kind of kid who would get in trouble spending way too much time partying and being an all around pain in the neck. Worst of all, he would pick on Aiden all the time, calling him names and just plain bullying him every chance he got. It reached the point where Aiden felt like he was falling apart. He couldn't sleep, he couldn't concentrate, had trouble eating and he couldn't feel comfortable around people anymore. If he had to rate his level of fear on a scale of one to ten he would have to say it was a nine or ten, in other words, intolerable.

If Aiden were to go to see a therapist, at first a recommendation would be made to see a medical doctor to decide whether or not medical treatment was needed. With any counseling whether it's ECT or some other form of therapy, professionals always want to make sure their patient's doctor is notified if they desire it. Some will say they do not want to do so, while others will say that's fine. The point is, competent therapists cover all of their bases first.

Since Aiden was a very intelligent boy, the chances would be good that he would be able to identify his authentic feelings pretty quickly in his first couple of months of therapy, along with the real cause of his stress. In ECT therapy, a brief examination of his life would point out to him that he was in control of most of his life. He was happy with his schoolwork, with his after-school job, and with his support group of friends. The relationship that was causing such debilitating fear, of course, was that with his stepbrother Jackson. Naturally, Aiden already knew that, but in therapy, he would learn how to appropriately release that fear. This might include identifying and making a list of all of the things that

CHAPTER THREE

were causing him fear and slowly working on reducing fear on each one.

Aiden and his therapist would also work on different techniques for reducing stress. For example, Aiden's penchant for fly-fishing would be excellent for this purpose. When Aiden was fishing, he felt that he was more in control of his life. Slowly over time, this would ease his level of tension and serve as a means of stress relaxation.

This wouldn't be ideal for everyone but it would work well in this boy's particular case. Why? Because when Aiden is out at the river fishing, he is able to let his mind wander. He daydreams and releases some of his fear-inducing feelings and sorts them out.

Of course, for Aiden as for anybody, there could never be any guarantees. Things do not always work out as planned. Imagine what it must be like for a young couple in their twenties who have a child. Maybe this will be you in just a few years. Instead of being born healthy, however, their child is born with a birth defect or heart defect. The first few years of the couple's relationship is spent at doctor's offices, not sleeping and excessive financial pain. Certainly none of this would have been in all of their happy plans of having a baby! The point is things change as you go forward. In Aiden's case he sought relief from excessive fear. By utilizing some of the ECT techniques used by all therapists to relieve stress, Aiden would stand a good chance of successfully distancing himself from his fear in the same way that Drew had in boot camp.

The difference between Aiden's case and Drew's was that Drew never had to go back to his relationship with stress. Boot camp was over and done. So Drew was able to leave therapy pretty whole. With our fictitious case of Aiden, his stepbrother Jackson would in all likelihood still be belligerent and would not want to himself go to therapy. Bullies like Jackson usually don't think they have a problem – though they clearly do. So as we examine Aiden's situation it is clear that his stepbrother had displayed power over Aiden whenever he could. Aiden felt helpless. In therapy, we would help Aiden to recognize that he needs to work on his own situation separate from his stepbrother. Spending as little time as possible with Jackson would be a big part of the solution.

Time would solve this problem eventually, because the day would come when Aiden would go off to college. Even then, however, Aiden should continue with therapy, as learning ECT would show him new and more varied ways to become calmer. For example writing, listening to music, and joining the chess club at school would all contribute to a lower level of tension and anxiety. Eventually, through the use of all of these techniques he should hopefully be able to lower his stress to a one or two.

With Emotional Core Therapy, the client has the power to enter and leave relationships. Aiden had spent years not fully understanding his emotions but he never needed professional help before. Now that he has learned how to monitor his body and his authentic feelings he will be able

CHAPTER THREE

to go on with his life because as he enters young adulthood he will already know how to identify his feelings, recognize toxic relationships and make smart choices to reduce stress. Therapists cannot make decisions for clients, the client has to make decisions about which relationships that they want to enter into. Sometimes people (like the fictional Aiden) have been in a toxic situation. The therapist's job is to be supportive within those situations and try to reduce the stress. The relief may not be instant, but it is in just about every case a step in the right direction.

Emotional Core Therapy is about being human and desiring to stay human. That means honoring and processing the four authentic feelings in all of life's situations. Let's say that there is a fifteen-year old girl named Charlene. She is the star of her school's soccer team. She loves the sport, so that should make her happy, right? Not necessarily. In this case it is actually making her miserable. Why? The pressure of always being the best, of always having to be the one who leads her team to victory, started getting to be too much for Charlene. The pressure was so stressful that she had trouble sleeping, trouble concentrating, had chest pains, mild tension – all of the classic signs of fear or stress. Her heart was beating fast. She had a fear of being a failure. In ECT therapy, it would quickly become apparent that her role on the soccer team was very demanding. Whether it was at practice or in an actual game, Charlene always felt that she was under a microscope. Her coach told Charlene that she was a "natural-born leader" and therefore gave her all kinds of responsibilities on the field. If one of the girls on the team wasn't playing well enough, Charlene was expected to find out why, take the girl under her wing, and improve her soccer skills. A tall order to say the least! At first Charlene liked all of the confidence that had been placed in her by her coach and her teammates, and even the parents and other spectators who attended the games. But after a while it became just too much pressure, and Charlene reached the point where she felt as though she could not take it anymore.

If Charlene were to enter into ECT therapy, one of the benefits would be that she and her therapist would compartmentalize Charlene's stress. She and her therapist would discuss the circumstances and more than likely a common theme would emerge: Charlene's persistent fear of not living up to everyone's expectations. The therapist would review Charlene's history, which would show that she was much more calm back when she was a younger kid. How did things change? One technique that is used in Emotional Core Therapy is to outline the patient's thoughts on a piece of paper, writing down five or maybe even ten different ways that Charlene felt overwhelmed each day. In therapy, Charlene would learn how to process her feelings and then she would be allowed to vent them. This almost always provides at least some momentary relief.

Of course, so long as Charlene remained on the soccer team, and the coach continued to see her as a "star," there would not be full relief. Charlene's stress level would remain

CHAPTER THREE

fairly high. Her situation was similar to Aiden's from our second example. Aiden still lived with Jackson, his annoying stepbrother, which was causing him fear. Both of these situations are relationships that these people entered into and they stayed with them, which is why their level of fear remained high. In a perfect world Jackson would have been shipped off to a juvenile detention center and Charlene would have quit the team and both would be happy. But in the real world she wouldn't do that because she cared too much about her coach and her teammates and she didn't want to let them down. Both Aiden and Charlene were stuck in their current circumstances and they were not going to be able to leave anytime soon. Nonetheless, in the short-term they would be able to work on some ECT techniques to effectively release their feelings.

Emotional Core Therapy does not promise utopia or a perfect outcome for every client. Let's keep it real, no therapy can offer that. Oftentimes the best you can do is to deal with your life's stresses head on in a more meaningful and manageable way. For Charlene, if she pursued ECT for a couple of months there is a good possibility that it would allow her to "reframe" her mental state. Instead of saying to herself, *I'm afraid, I'm scared, I'm not doing enough, I'm going to screw up and make my team lose,* Emotional Core Therapy would help Charlene to develop a different mindset. Her frame of thinking would be more like this: *I'm only one part of the team, and I'm doing my part well. My heart is in the right place, it's the pressure to succeed that's causing me excessive fear. I need to recognize that there is more to life than just soccer.* In other words, Charlene needs to create some separation between herself and this sport.

Through ECT we can learn common techniques to reduce stress. For example, Charlene's therapist might suggest for her to practice meditation before games as a way to reclaim herself. One very effective way of practicing meditation is to pay attention to your "calm self." For example, Charlene could review what she did before she became the school's big soccer star that helped her to be peaceful. Working on a calm, steady way to breathe might be one technique. Taking deep short breaths, helps to slow a person's thought processes down. Just plopping down in front of the TV and watching a silly sitcom or mindless "reality show" prior to a soccer game might help Charlene to relax as well. These techniques would help her to slow her body down and clear her mind. ECT would teach Charlene how to monitor her body and start to become calmer.

Keep in mind what Emotional Core Therapy can and cannot do. First and foremost, it helps people to regain their "humanness." But it can never cure cancer, solve all of your problems, or give you all the answers. No therapy can promise these results. Every new relationship we enter into with people, places and things will cause a response from us as human beings. It will either bring joy or fear. That's simply the way life works. With ECT, however, it can be a happier and more peaceful life, and one that we can live with greater dignity and independence. No one can really predict the future, all we can do is work on releasing feelings and obtaining a meditative state of calmness.

Another very common source of stress is the workplace. This can certainly be true for teens as well as for adults. Workplace stress (or school stress) can vary from person to person depending on many factors. Think of jobs that adults have such as a postman or deliveryman. If the person in this job has an injury or condition with his feet and the job requires walking all day, this job would cause excessive stress. What if another individual has no health problems and enjoys nature, being outside, and helping people. In stark contrast, he may love the job. Two different people, same job, yet different levels of stress. That's because people experience stress differently. Still, if you examine the most stressful jobs in our society, most of them cause excessive fear on a normal human's emotions. Look no further than a soldier, policeman, ironworker, professional football player, or a stay at home mother of five, and you will see a common variable. Most of these jobs require a great deal of tasks to be completed, usually in uncomfortable conditions. Thus, they lead to very high levels of stress.

To more closely examine teen workplace stress, let's look at another hypothetical case that we can learn from. This one involves a Junior in high school named Tyler. He stayed busy all day long, both at school and then after school and on weekends working at his father's hardware store. Tyler grew up in a close knit family and he felt a sense of obligation to the family business. But the pressure of putting in so many hours under the watchful (and often critical) eye of his father was getting to Tyler. He was worried about making a mistake that might hurt the business, and he dreaded the idea of disappointing his father. He was also fearful about not having enough money for college if he cut back on his hours on the store. This young man had devoted his life to his family and now it was falling apart.

Tyler exhibited several of the classic symptoms of anxiety: he had trouble sleeping, muscle tension, and he lost weight. With Emotional Core Therapy, Tyler would be encouraged to compartmentalize all of his excessive fears. We would write down each fear and discuss the situation in detail. Part of Tyler' excessive fear was financial stress. He wanted to go to a leading university, but the costs of tuition were staggering. Was the future that he had always dreamed of realistically within his reach? These were not entirely rational thoughts, they were just excessive fears in case the situation went bad.

Over the course of several months of using ECT, Tyler would need to make some key decisions to help bring down his high level of fear. For example, one idea might be to sit down for a serious talk with his father about cutting back on his working hours, explaining to his dad how he could be a more valuable worker if he could just have a little bit more free time to rest and relax. That way he would be less tired and therefore not as worried about messing something up. He might also look into financial aid and scholarships and

CHAPTER THREE

discover that paying for college will not be as unreachable as he had feared. In other words, ECT would help give Tyler perspective on the whole process of balancing his current work obligations and future college ambitions. He would still be able to work but he would also have to grieve the loss of a certain amount of income. The good news is, identifying this grief would provide Tyler relief from a fearful point of view in that he could rest assured that there would still be a way for him to attend the college of his choice. This relief will lower Tyler's position on the fear scale, maybe dropping it from an eight or nine down to a five or six in a couple of months, and hopefully even lower a few months later.

All therapists want what is best for their clients. But just remember that they can't promise to predict what the future holds in store for you. Tyler would still have to work through his fear and loss, and there is no telling how long that might take. The point is every situation is different. As we have seen with other situations in this book, sometimes the road to recovery can be long and hard. Fortunately, Emotional Core Therapy offers a path, a strategy for coping that helps us not only with major crises, but also with the less drastic (but every bit as real) worries and stressors that all of us contend with in our everyday lives.

Hopefully the "FEAR" you have about comprehending this approach has been alleviated somewhat after reading the anxiety chapter. Feel free to glance at the adjacent flowchart to measure your comprehension of the psychological process we are teaching in this book. Don't worry (otherwise known as fear) if you haven't mastered the entire approach just yet. We will revisit the approach in more detail in the following chapter, "Using ECT to Understand Anger."

5 Step ECT Flow Chart

| Relationships; self, other people, places, things |

⇩

| Four Authentic Feelings; joy, grief, fear, relief |

⇩

| Uncomfortable Symptoms; muscle tightness, fatigue, etc. |

⇩

| Releasing Process; learn to discharge toxic feelings |

⇩

| Balancing Your Equilibrium; practice various daily meditative techniques |

CHAPTER THREE

List Five Relationships That You Have Entered That Have Caused You Fear

A) TAKING THE SAT EXAM

B) GOING ON A ROLLER COASTER.

1.
2.
3.
4.
5.

Notes:

List Five Ways You Can Release Debilitating Feelings Of Fear.

A) READ COMIC BOOKS OR SOMETHING FUNNY

B) CALL AN OLD FRIEND WHO HAS MOVED AWAY AND CATCH UP ON STUFF

1.
2.
3.
4.
5.

Notes:

CHAPTER THREE

SYMPTOMS OF ANXIETY

HAVING AN INCREASED HEART RATE

BREATHING RAPIDLY (HYPERVENTILATION)

FEELING POWERLESS

HAVING A SENSE OF IMPENDING DANGER, PANIC OR DOOM

FEELING APPREHENSIVE

SWEATING

FEELING WEAK OR FATIGUED

TREMBLING

List Five Of Your Own Symptoms Of Anxiety

1.
2.
3.
4.
5.

Notes:

CHAPTER FOUR
Using ECT To Understand Anger

So far, we've mostly been exploring situations where someone has hurt our feelings or harmed us in some way. But as I am sure that you will admit, on occasion you too have had episodes when you lose your temper and get angry with other people, sometimes in a way that may be hurtful. We all have done so from at one point or another. That doesn't make you a bad person. It just means that we all have faults in relationships. There are instances when we accidentally or intentionally hurt others in our lives. Examples might be inappropriately talking back to your parents, using force to intimidate other kids at school, or telling mean jokes at somebody else's expense.

All of us do something like this at least once in a while. The difference, however, between an emotionally healthy person and an abusive person is that the emotionally healthy person truly regrets doing the hurtful or harmful act. Why? They know that hurting someone is destructive in nature.

Have you ever heard the saying, "Treat others as you want to be treated"? It really makes a lot of sense if you think about it, and this same sense of fairness and respect for others can be seen using the techniques of Emotional Core Therapy. With ECT we understand that it is entering and leaving relationships that causes stress (otherwise known as debilitating feelings of fear and grief). As we discussed earlier in the book, when we go towards a relationship we like (such as a good friend) there is joy. When we leave something we like (for example, that same good friend) there is grief. When we go towards something we dislike (for instance, taking an exam that we did not prepare for) there is fear. When we leave something we dislike (finishing the exam and receiving a decent grade on it) there is relief. Since anger is a reaction to grief, what relationship is being stressed? The answer is the relationship that you have with yourself. In the hypothetical cases you will read in this chapter keep in mind that each character who is angry is really grieving his own sense of loss. That is the important point that I want you to keep in time.

We all from time to time have made mistakes that hurt others and brought grief or fear into others' lives. Examples might include arguing with your parents, or "blowing up" at your friends at school. The difference is that when you begin to honor your authentic feelings of joy, grief, fear, and relief, you become aware of your uncomfortable muscle and bodily sensations that result from stress. This physical discomfort is a signal that something is wrong with a relationship. With ECT, we recognize that our normal state of being is one of meditation or relaxation. Hence, we become trained to eliminate the debilitating feelings of fear and loss.

Anger is a reaction to grief. People who are angry are in fact, grieving and suffering loss. Each individual varies in their intensity and duration of anger. One of the benefits of using ECT is it helps give us a better grasp of authentic feelings, so we can dig deeper and get to the real roots of someone's anger. We must also realize that anger can affect the central nervous system, so it's important especially as we get older to have less stress on the body, and less anger in one's life. By having less anger and stress, your blood pressure can stay calm and your body can be more regulated.

Let's take the fictional example of an angry sixteen year old boy to see how ECT can help him better his communication skills and in turn get his needs met. The young man in this hypothetical case, Connor, often loses his temper with his twelve-year old brother, Ethan. "You moron! I already showed you how to do that math problem three times, stop asking me to help you again you dummy." Wow! Can't you just feel the harmful and destructive power of those words as you read them?

With Emotional Core Therapy, Connor would be taught to honor himself as well as others. A better way of stating his grief of constantly be asked the same homework questions over and over by his little brother might be by saying something like this: "Ethan, I am really unhappy when I have to keep repeating stuff. I'm disappointed because I know how smart you are. But you're just using my answers to finish your homework instead of really learning the math the way that you are supposed to learn it." It doesn't have to be these exact words, but something that conveys this sentiment in a similar non-accusatory yet frankly honest manner. These kinds of words would be much more likely to draw Connor's little brother into a conversation that might actually solve the problem. In stark contrast, by Connor getting angry and sarcastic, the two of them will just end up fighting and misunderstanding each other even more. The more authentic these two brothers can be with each other, the closer they will become in their relationship. As people become better at authenticating their four feelings of joy, grief, fear, and relief, they can learn to grow their relationships further and better.

ECT would probably not only help Connor to get along better with Ethan, it would help him to evolve as a human being too. It would allow him to use more authentic words such as "unhappy" and "disappointed" instead of "moron" and "dummy." These words should help Connor to get in touch with his inner self. The sooner he gets in touch with his core feelings, the sooner he can release them and move on to a healthier state of being. The beauty of ECT is the ability to make the hundreds of feelings simplified into one of the four authentic feelings. By doing so, one has a much better chance of releasing psychic pain and moving on from the negative state of being.

CHAPTER FOUR

As Connor becomes more emotionally centered, there is less chance that he will turn to the use of anger, as anger is nothing more than a reaction to one of the four authentic feelings. When you learn to live in a more authentic way, honoring your feelings, you become less inclined to need anger as a response to relationships. Why would one use anger as a means of communication when there are far better, less destructive options available?

Our next example of anger is the hypothetical case of a fourteen-year old girl named Nancy, who is the youngest of four children. Her mother is a single mom who works hard, but the family always seems to be struggling to make ends meet financially. That means Nancy gets a lot of hand-me-down clothes from her older sisters rather than the cool new designer fashions that many of her friends are always wearing. One day when Nancy asks her mom for money to buy this awesome new pair of jeans she saw at the mall, her mother gently explains that they are too expensive. Turned down again! Nancy explodes in a fit of anger. "That's so unfair, Mom! All my friends dress like supermodels and I have to wear dorky Old School clothes that make me look like such a dweeb! Why are we always so broke?"

Of course, later on Nancy feels terrible about how insensitive she was when she blew up at her mom. She loves her mother very much and feels awful that she can't control her anger. Using ECT, we would examine the situation for the four authentic feelings. Anger is not one of the four authentic feelings, so what was Nancy really feeling? Nancy had obviously been very hurt when she heard the bad news that once again she would have to settle for second best when it came to clothing. Her feeling of grief came from her perception that maybe this time, somehow things would be different. In her mind she had envisioned asking her mother for the money for the new jeans, and her mother saying that yes, she was going to let her daughter buy whatever she wanted this time. But what she was really grieving was the loss of feeling respected by all of her classmates. Nancy felt like everyone thought that her family was some kind of "poverty case," and she was sad and embarrassed about it. Simply put, Nancy was deeply hurt, but she did not know how to process her feelings appropriately.

Let's examine how Nancy could approach this situation if she had learned about Emotional Core Therapy and using the four authentic feelings. She might say, "Hi, Mom, I want to talk to you about something. I know that you've been kinda down and having a tough time with money, and it's been making me sad and upset too. But I have an idea for buying some new clothes I saw at the mall. I can save up half of the money from babysitting and maybe you can give me the other half?"

This alternative approach would be much better than saying, "That's so unfair, Mom! Why are we always so broke?" With this new statement, Nancy is acknowledging her mother's circumstances and also her own authentic feelings. "Sad"

CHAPTER FOUR

and "upset" are really just different ways to describe grief. That is why in the second example where Nancy shares her feelings with her mother, Nancy had a better chance of drawing her mom into the conversation and they just might end up actually understanding each other for a change.

Anger pulls people away from each other and injects fear into the dialogue and it detracts from healthy communication with other human beings. In the long run, Nancy will have a much better relationship with her mom if she can encourage meaningful conversations with her rather than losing her temper and making both of them upset.

Another hypothetical example of someone using anger inappropriately involves Franklin, a high school senior who is on the verge of breaking up with Christie, his longtime girlfriend. Bitter, angry and jealous, Franklin has lashed out verbally at Christie, calling her all kinds of terrible names, including in front of other people. He (falsely) accused her of "running around" and branded her a "tramp."

This hate-fueled behavior was not at all like Franklin's typical demeanor, which was usually carefree and easygoing. What went wrong? What might be the true root of all of that anger? What was the source of his anger? In Emotional Core Therapy, Franklin and his therapist would find out more about his past and how it related to what was currently going on his life. For example, did his sense of self-esteem and self-value come from having a girlfriend? If so, potentially losing Christie would be even more traumatic for him than a breakup would be otherwise. In fact, the sense of loss might be downright unbearable.

The key to recovery would be for Franklin to begin to process his feelings more and more. Rather than dwell on the loss, it would be important for him to acknowledge it and then to properly "mourn" it. In these kinds of cases, further examination of one's authentic feelings often reveals some hard truths that a person may have been reluctant to admit to prior to therapy. For example, it might come out that Franklin's treatment of his girlfriend had been less than kind for a very long time, in fact, long before their breakup became imminent. He would always act possessive and jealous whenever she was around other boys, even though clearly it was completely innocent on her part. In other words, his own insecurities and fears about his own shortcomings were getting the better of Franklin and basically turning him into a mean and controlling bully.

With ECT, Franklin's therapist would help him to recognize that he had a powerful sense of loss when it came to his relationship with Christie. He would then be able to begin to honor his feelings and change his vocabulary. For example, he might start to use statements like, "I feel grief when my feelings are not respected," or, "I feel a sense of loss when it seems like I'm not appreciated." He could also begin to change his behaviors that were causing him grief and loss, and to show Christie more respect too.

As therapists we are trained to look for growth. But it's important to note that the exact amount of growth always

CHAPTER FOUR

varies from one person to the next. Some clients want to learn all that they can to get better. If ECT was learning the alphabet, some clients would want to learn from A to Z, while others would only want to learn A through P. Therapy has to be supportive of each client no matter what state of life they are in.

Let's consider another fictitious case of a young person with anger issues who could benefit from ECT. This time it involves a nineteen-year old boy named Raoul. Fleeing a life of poverty in Guatemala, Raoul arrived in New York City alone on his eighteenth birthday. He quickly got a job at a fast food restaurant, and by being such a hard worker, he soon became the manager, in charge of a mostly teenage kitchen crew. Raoul worked very long hours in the hot kitchen and he became very harsh with the kids who worked for him, yelling at them for even the smallest of mistakes. He was especially tough on a timid new employee named Valerie. Raoul would call her names, devalue her role as a worker and belittle her in front of the other employees.

What might be behind this kind of obnoxious behavior? We would explore that question in Emotional Core Therapy and we might find, for example, that being verbally harsh and demanding gave Raoul a sense of power and control that was lacking in other areas of his life. Maybe he had very few friends or even acquaintances outside of work. In other words, he had no support system. One of the first things the ECT therapist would do would be to start the process of releasing Raoul's feelings. It may be that he had never had an opportunity to tell anyone how he felt deep inside, especially how fearful he felt. Alone in a new country, he had a sense that he was considered "at the bottom of the totem pole." He did not speak English very well and often felt like an outsider. This led to feelings of frustration that he vented onto those around him in angry outbursts.

Through counseling in ECT, Raoul would begin to heal his relationship with Valerie and all of the other people who worked under him. But ECT would do this by helping Raoul to realize certain things about himself. For starters, he would be encouraged to make friends outside of work. This way the kids at the restaurant wouldn't be the only people in his life. Once he had more friends, Raoul would be able to authentically share how he was feeling. He could share his deeper feelings of loss and grief.

Over time, Raoul would recognize that he would need to work as hard as he could on being authentic with his feelings, as that would be the key to keeping his anger under control. Emotional Core Therapy would also help him to recognize that being lonely was something that he could change.

The goal of ECT as with any therapy is to make you more independent and empowered. Identifying one's feelings in therapy is a big step forward, but it's even more important to make this become a part of your everyday life. The more you have support and friends the less you will be alone. This would help someone like Raoul to identify and understand that his displays of anger were really expressions of loss and grief. He could then begin to monitor his feelings of anger each day. For example, every time he would start to feel angry he would ask himself, what am I losing? What am I grieving?

In Emotional Core Therapy, Raoul's therapist would look at his previous history to help him find ways to relax and release his feelings. This could involve outdoor activities such as bike riding or maybe he could take up a hobby such as painting, especially if that was something that he had done in the past that he found relaxing. Journaling and writing can also be used to help release the toxic pain of loss, as a person like Raoul probably feels like he left a lot behind in his home country trying to make a new life for himself in America. These kinds of pent up feelings can easily lead to excessive anger. Once Raoul learns to release his feelings in an authentic and healthy manner, and he will start to feel more comfortable with himself. All of these techniques would very likely improve his communication style, which in turn would make him a better boss at work – somebody that the other workers would like and respect rather than fear and loathe.

Over many years of doing therapy, I am constantly reminded of the humanness of all of us. In my private practice setting, I usually don't work with the serious or profoundly emotionally disturbed. Yet I do have clients who come to me with a wide range of mental health conditions. Some clients who seek treatment have been classified or diagnosed in their past as having Attention Deficit Disorder, BiPolar Disorder, Narcissistic Disorder and Obsessive Disorder. Others have sought treatment for self-mutilation issues such as cutting themselves. Some clients have suffered sexual trauma and sexual dysfunction issues. In my experience, ECT can help a broad spectrum of these types of mental health issues that are mild in scope when used with other therapy techniques besides ECT. Why? ECT utilizes core techniques that are common to most humans. For example, who has not suffered feelings of loss or fear? Who cannot benefit from learning various relaxation techniques? When would learning how to release feelings be detrimental to a client?

What I have found is that I utilize many different techniques (other than ECT) for clients that have more moderate to severe personality problems. This is primarily because of resistance to change. Oftentimes you need a variety of psychological techniques to help the more resistant client to grow. In many cases, more energy and focus is needed to bring about positive outcomes with clients who are suffering serious mental health issues. Serious cases of depression, anxiety, and anger would likely benefit from a similar approach for the same reason.

One of the awesome results of learning ECT is that it makes you realize that no one gets a free ride in life if they aspire to stay healthy and human. You can't kill, steal, or harm someone else, without feeling guilty (in other words, having a sense of loss). Why? The feelings of loss will stay inside you and not be released. Remember, the key point of ECT is to live in a meditative and relaxed state of being. In order to do ECT properly one has to monitor and release all four authentic feelings on a daily basis. Being stuck in a state of grief can be a real drag.

Earlier in the book we discussed how you could gauge someone's success in learning Emotional Core Therapy. The more you can learn and acquire the steps of the ECT flowchart the more confident you will feel about yourself. This book is not about becoming a leader, gaining fame or fortune. Most of the people who assume high levels of responsibility also have high levels of stress (otherwise known as fear). They have excessive fear because they have too many responsibilities and too many tasks.

I want my clients to have power, and to be able to handle their responsibilities without excessive fear or stress. ECT allows clients to get a grasp on what they can and can't handle when it comes to various situations in life, and this is true regardless of your age. Oftentimes, when someone is overly fearful or stressed, anger comes out. The more you become comfortable with the ECT process, the less chance you will become angry. That's because you learn to process your feelings better. Since anger is not an authentic feeling anyway, there becomes less of a need to use anger. Emotionally healthy people can express feelings of sadness, just as readily as feelings of joy. The point is, they are being true to themselves, which is precisely what makes them emotionally healthy in the first place.

5 Step ECT Flow Chart

Relationships;
self, other people, places, things

⇩

Four Authentic Feelings;
joy, grief, fear, relief

⇩

Uncomfortable Symptoms;
muscle tightness, fatigue, etc.

⇩

Releasing Process;
learn to discharge toxic feelings

⇩

Balancing Your Equilibrium;
practice various daily meditative techniques

CHAPTER FOUR

List five relationships / events that have caused you anger (which is a reaction to grief)

A) SOMEONE CHEATING WHEN YOU'RE PLAYING A SPORT

B) SOMEONE TELLING YOU TO "SHUT UP"

1.
2.
3.
4.
5.

Notes:

List five ways that allow you to appropriately process your anger (which is a reaction to grief)

A) I FEEL SAD WHEN YOU DEMAND MY TIME AND ENERGY WITHOUT SAYING THANK YOU.

B) I AM HURT (ANOTHER WORD FOR GRIEF) THAT YOU BORROW MY MONEY WITHOUT PAYING ME BACK.

1.
2.
3.
4.
5.

Notes:

CHAPTER FOUR

SYMPTOMS OF ANGER

FEELING HOT AND FLUSHED

RACING HEARTBEAT

TENSION IN SHOULDERS AND NECK

FEELING AGITATED

List Five Of Your Own Symptoms Of Anger

1.
2.
3.
4.
5.

Notes:

CHAPTER FIVE
Using ECT to Help Couples

As we begin to discuss how Emotional Core Therapy can help couples, I want to highlight an important reason why everyone would benefit from using ECT. Especially if you were brought up in one of the colder areas of the country, you probably remember how your parents were on your case making sure that you dress warm during the winter. Now that you are older you know what their reason was. Protection. You can get sick and be subjected to long term damage when you are out in the cold for long periods of time without adequate protection. In much the same way, you can think of Emotional Core Therapy as an ideal way of protecting yourself from the inevitable harm that accompanies the arrival of debilitating stress. Whether you like it or not, you will suffer fear and loss in your life. In fact, most of us will have at least some minor irritation on a daily or weekly basis. On a larger scale, you are old enough now to take a serious look at our world and see that it is full of problems that cause people all kinds of traumatic states of fear and grief. I'm not trying to be bleak or pessimistic, just realistic about the challenges facing you as an individual and your generation collectively.

Emotional Core Therapy can help you to meet those challenges head on. It is an easy to use technique (once you understand it) technique for protecting human beings from the "harmful cold weather" known as stress. I believe that education is the key. People realize that emotional trauma is a national epidemic but no one knows how to fix the problem. When I see the hundreds of psychology books for sale that take an advanced degree to comprehend, it becomes clear why a solution has not been found. There needs to be a self-help book that every literate person can read. To that extent, I have tried at great lengths to keep this ECT book reader friendly.

As we begin this chapter on couples we will again see how ECT can bring "joy" to your life, in this case by helping you with love relationships. Nearly all of us know the story of Romeo and Juliet. They had deep and eternal love. It seemed like the two lovebirds never failed to keep the spark or chemistry going in their relationship, no matter what difficulties came between them. The only problem with this love tragedy is that it is not very realistic. That is where Emotional Core Therapy steps in. It shows us how two people can build a realistic partnership better by using better communication patterns.

Before I discuss a few (mostly hypothetical) scenarios where ECT helped young couples navigate through their lives, I want to point out that I see lots of people in therapy that seem very happy with their lives being single. Being "in a relationship" is not some sort of automatic guarantee of perfect, trouble-free happiness. As a matter of fact, there are even benefits to remaining single for a period of time. You get to know to learn and love yourself without having the demands of a partner on a daily basis. Still, others recognize that they have a better chance of getting all of their needs met through a committed relationship. Since ECT deals with authentic feelings, there is no difference in treatment of couples of various ethnicities, heterosexual or homosexual. Emotional, financial, spiritual, and physical needs as we already know vary from person to person. I've discovered the benefits of focusing on authentic feelings in a relationship takes away from biases of both the client and therapists.

In this chapter we begin to see more clearly what brings us stress in our relationships from the perspective of both young men and young women. It is the "needs" and "demands" that each partner brings to the relationship that cause us to have one of the four authentic feelings. In our ECT Flowchart, we see that needs are broken down to four areas. These are emotional, financial, spiritual, and physical. We have organized needs into these four areas because they provide a simple structure for us to understand what causes us stress. There are literally millions of stresses in relationships. Don't worry, I'm not going to discuss every single one of them! For the sake of simplicity we break them down into one of four areas.

The first couple I want to discuss is Blake and Jenny. This hypothetical couple were seniors in high school who had been dating fairly seriously for about a year. In the last few months, though, things had been going downhill fast an they found themselves arguing more often than not. Blake never seemed to listen to Jenny's concerns. Her family was not as well off financially as Blake's family, and she was worried about going to a good college next year. Blake on the other hand only wanted to party and have fun in his senior year of high school, rather than worrying about more serious things in the future.

Things started to go from bad to worse when Jenny told Blake that she thought they should end their relationship. Blake was stunned and insisted that they should remain a couple. If they both agreed to see a therapist to find out if they could work out their problems and stay together, ECT might be able to help them. Therapy would reveal that Jenny's statement of emotional pain regarding her future was clearly based on her authentic feelings of grief. She was grieving the ideal of a financially secure college career along with a strong and potentially lasting relationship with Blake. In addition, she had a lot of fear regarding her future: wonder if she had to settle for a second rate college? How much might that damage her career?

The focus of the treatment with both Jenny and Blake would be to highlight the authentic feelings of fear and loss that Jenny faced. By listening to her processing her feelings

CHAPTER FIVE

it started to become apparent that there was more than one way Jenny felt loss and fear. She was also grieving the potential loss of ever attaining her ideal job, a happy relationship with Blake and most of all, Jenny was grieving the loss of a young man who cared and listened to her.

Using ECT, it would likely also become apparent that Blake had difficulty emotionally connecting with girls. Despite his outwardly cocky personality, deep inside he was insecure about his own shortcomings and worried that he could never live up to Jenny's high standards and expectations. He was running away from the future rather than facing it head on.

If I were helping a couple like this, I would have them make a list of what each needed at different levels (emotional, financial, spiritual and physical) from each other. We would then discuss on a weekly basis, the efforts to meet each partner's needs, spending equal time in therapy stressing each person's needs, and not being just one sided. In other words, we would spend half the time on Jenny and half on Blake. Successful relationships are the result of mature couples meeting each other's needs. Of course, couples in high school all have some more maturing to do, and this almost certainly would be a contributing factor in Jenny and Blake's problems. Blake was used to basically living as a kid and just was not ready to start concerning himself with adult problems and issues. Yet this was not what Jenny needed at all. Blake had difficulty really paying attention to the emotional feeling of loss that Sue was displaying on a daily basis. He also had difficulty relating to her excessive fear. ECT would likely reveal that Blake continually tried to hide himself in partying and lots of fun stuff to escape his authentic feelings of grief.

In order to receive any benefit from therapy, Jenny would need to assert her feelings. It would be important for both of them to spend time working hard on making sure each other's feelings were heard, in the authentic feelings of joy, grief, fear and relief.

Emotional Core Therapy could be successful for both Jenny and Blake if they could both learn to understand and respect each other's authentic feelings. Most critically, Jenny would need to rid herself of toxic feelings of loss and grief. As for Blake, he was truly happy in his relationship except for not being able to please Jenny. He really didn't have a lot of excess needs himself that needed to be met so in therapy they would be able to focus a lot on alleviating Jenny's pain.

Emotional Core Therapy can give hope to a couple in therapy, as it matches authentic feelings with the needs of partners. Most couples can learn a process of being authentic in their feelings by using ECT. When ECT is used with couples, it can bring them closer together and they both can learn at the same time the different techniques of ECT. In other words, they both can help each learn it in addition to the therapist helping them. As a relationship builds, ECT is also helpful in building independence for both partners, which is always especially important for young people. They both can work on finding peace for themselves, a vital component for all healthy relationships. When you have peace in your life and you work on it every day, you start to work on vitality and vigor which is basically a sign of power. We want both partners in therapy to have as much power as they want and to feel as vibrant as possible. That only comes from being emotionally balanced.

Examining each relationship through the eyes of Emotional Core Therapy, we see that healthy relationships honor the four authentic feelings of joy, grief, fear, and relief. A healthy relationship recognizes that the individual may need space to relax and have time for himself/herself. When you can finally begin to understand this key point of ECT, you can begin to have "real and authentic" power. Power you can count on long-term. Relationships that last a long time.

The second couple I would like to highlight is a young couple named Jeff and Kim, recent college graduates who decided to live together before getting married. The names have been changed but their story is true. Both were very energetic and optimistic young people. They were both successful at work and had a great group of friends. Both were very popular in the office and their respective workplaces. They were both quite attracted to each other and obviously very committed to each other. So what could possibly be wrong that such a vibrant and strong young couple would need to see a marital therapist? Why would they blow up and get so mad at each from time to time? How would ECT be able to help them?

The main issue that Jeff and Kim faced was that when they disagreed on something it would always result in a loud blowout fight. They could be very affectionate with each other one minute and swearing and yelling at each other the next. They were both extremely perplexed as to why this occurred and they didn't realize it themselves. Jeff and Kim were obviously very popular and successful irrespective of each other. Prior to their relationships both of them were happy go lucky individuals, both were athletic in high school and hung around with the in crowd. They each had supportive families and were financially secure. Both were upstanding, law abiding citizens with good intentions for their lives. At the core of the couple's dispute was the problem that being a couple means that you have to share. You have to compromise with the other person's point of view.

As a therapist I would hope that my young clients indeed, all my clients, would be as optimistic and energetic as Jeff and Kim were in their everyday lives. The real problem with Jeff and Kim's relationship was that they jumped in very quickly to becoming lovers with each other. When they lived separately they yearned for each other. The attraction was so powerful that they leapt into getting an apartment and began to live as a couple. Instead of spending weekends apart from each other and missing each other they were now together each day. As I explained to the young couple they just needed to find a healthy balance of time spent with each other and apart from each other. Over the years I've found that regardless of age, sex or ethnicity, all couples have to work on having an emotionally healthy self, separate from a relationship with their partner. A good relationship exists when both individuals respect themselves but also support the process that a true partnership provides.

As a metaphor, I used two magnets with opposite energies. When two magnets are far apart they seek each other out. But when the magnets are too close they repel. This is just like couples do when they initially meet. When two people are too close together they repel. And they will wait for each other. It would be ideal to have a magnetic energy that was perfectly in balance all the time. But that is not realistic of life. As ECT tells us, all relationships are either growing toward us or moving away. These relationships evoke feelings in us such as joy, grief, fear and relief. All young couples including Kim and Jeff are excited and motivated to begin a relationship with their new partner. Why? It's a chance for joy. What is joy? Happiness and pleasure. We all want that authentic feeling and we are trained as kids to pursue it. You are told to save money in a piggy bank when you are little. Why? You will be able to buy things that you enjoy when you are older. Study hard in school. Why? You'll be able to get a job when you are older so you can buy new things. Or live a life with good resources.

Young people like to watch romance or love movies. Why? Everyone hopes to meet Prince Charming or a perfect girl. Eternal joy, however, is a myth that in most cases is broken quite quickly once couples start living together. Healthy relationships are usually the result of two adults committed to working on a relationship. The key is the word "work," which means time. It takes work and effort to see the other person's point of view. It takes time to learn the emotional, financial, spiritual and physical needs of a partner. The healthier relationships that I see are those where both partners really appreciate the benefit of having a partner and desire to work toward making their partner happy. That's what real maturity is, a recognition that yes I could live my life single and survive every day. The reader may ask what makes somebody want to work on a relationship with a partner. The answer is really no different than a job or career. Oftentimes people are motivated to find a job because they need money. They may initially be motivated by fear of being poor and having few resources. Others may be motivated by joy, they may have so much joy in what they are doing that they make a career out of it.

Relationships with a partner are usually motivated by the same authentic feelings of joy and fear. With Kim and Jeff it was obvious that they had a great deal of joy motivating them to be together. But the real problem with both of these young people was that they were not used to working on a relationship on a day to day level on the four aspects of emotional, financial, spiritual and physical needs. In other words, because they jumped in so quickly they had more demands placed on them and they were overwhelmed and not used to it.

With ECT we came across certain things about the relationship with Kim and Jeff. They both had to change addresses

CHAPTER FIVE

and move and this costs money. They both had to pay for a wedding and this cost money. They had to spend more time with each other each day so they had to listen to each other more. They both had different views of religion, which meant compromise. They both had different needs physically so they had to learn a great deal about each other in a short amount of time. All of this was overwhelming to them and caused an excessive amount of fear.

When we examined Jeff and Kim's new life using Emotional Core Therapy we were able to see that they had started their relationship very quickly which led to each of them having excessive fear. Jeff was feeling afraid that he might abandon Kim because he couldn't deal with living with a woman so young in his life. He was afraid that he couldn't deal with all the drama and emotions. Kim was feeling equally fearful that she would not be able to handle all of the household chores that she felt obligated to do. She wasn't sure that she would be able to get a handle on it and take care of a man.

Over the course of several months we examined all of the four authentic feelings involved with Jeff and Kim. They were able to see that they would need to make minor adjustments and compromises for each of their needs, so that they could balance their life a little bit better. There was a reassuring feeling by both of them that they could work through their marital relationship to change their lives. The ECT approach was helpful with both Kim and Jeff as they were both able to recognize their individual feelings and work toward a resolution.

One of the key things that they both did very well in therapy was to learn to relax and spend some time by themselves each day. This was so they could calm themselves down.

Much like learning to swim or ride a bike, learning to express one's feelings is a process. At the core of the process is externalizing our feelings versus internalizing them. In simple terms, externalizing one's feelings means to put something outside of the mind. In other words the release of fear or a thought. Internalizing means to incorporate within oneself. There are good things to internalize-values, ethics, homework, anything learned-however, toxic fears are unhealthy for the mind and body. These negative stored feelings are not really healthy to keep in and they cause stress. Oftentimes people who store their feelings repeatedly have body function problems such as muscular tension, hands trembling, sweating, shaking and nightmares. Not only are these feelings uncomfortable they are unhealthy.

Jeff and Kim were able to work through the major relationship changes in their lives in a short period of time because they truly saw the benefit or having a partner and the joy it could bring. ECT was helpful to both of them as they were both able to recognize their individual feelings and work toward a resolution.

A person has to be fully capable of giving in a relationship to a partner. Let's look at all four aspects of one's needs in a relationship in a hypothetical case. This scenario involves a very healthy young lady who was vibrant successful and full of life. She meets someone like Jeff from our first example but in this case the young man gets in a car accident soon after they get together. He has surgery, loses his job and is in a lot of pain. The point is no one can predict the future or predict how relationships will work out in the future. This is all the more reason to focus on authentic feelings as a therapist and also for our clients. As we focus more on authentic feelings we move towards a better resolution and there are less surprises and less shock in one's life. With ECT we have an equal responsibility of listening to each other's needs. Meditation and relaxation are hallmarks of emotionally healthy people. Many successful people learn to balance their workplace and family responsibilities with ways to relax. As long as one can daydream and keep reflective one can let their mind relax. It doesn't have to be sitting in a yoga position or listening to your body. There are other ways to do it.

The real reason why Emotional Core Therapy is a game changer in the field of psychology is the ability for the client to "transfer" the invaluable techniques learned in this book to new relationships. For example, when you enter ECT therapy to deal with an overbearing boyfriend or girlfriend who overwhelms you to exhaustion, you learn some basic tools to protect yourself. You learn how to identify fear, feel the symptoms of fear, process those feelings, and work towards a meditative state. Once you learn a meditative state, it is easier to identify future feelings of fear with your boyfriend or girlfriend. You can then utilize these ECT techniques that you have learned to change your behavior so that you don't continue to experience these feelings over and over again. Also, you can then use these invaluable techniques to help with other relationship problems such as a domineering parent or a disrespectful friend.

Let's look at a hypothetical example of something like this in simple terms. A high school couple, Benny and Shauna, go out on a date every Friday night. Usually a movie, maybe a concert, whatever it is, always something fun. The only problem is, whenever Benny comes over to Shauna's house to pick her up, he has to wait, sometimes as much as an hour, because she is still in the bathroom "getting ready" for their date. Before long Benny begins to feels hurt and disrespected by his girlfriend. He also is very anxious about being late for whatever event he had planned for them. His authentic feelings of fear and grief affect Benny very negatively. He becomes agitated, experiences muscle tension, and even begins to lose hope. These symptoms have to be released somehow.

If Benny were to use ECT, he would discover that it is the "relationship" he has entered into that is causing him stress. He would be encouraged to change his behavior by discussing the issues with Shauna. They would change how they schedule their dates, with Shauna beginning her "preparation" time earlier in the evening so that she would be ready when Benny arrives for their date. This would make Benny begin to feel empowered in the relationship, and he would be able to release his authentic feelings of fear and grief in a constructive manner with his girlfriend, which in turn would help him to regain his normal, peaceful and meditative state.

Let's take the story a little bit further and say that now, two weeks later Benny has similar feelings of fear and grief when the coach on his baseball team shuffles Benny to last place in the batting order. The young man would be able to utilize the same ECT techniques he learned with his girlfriend to deal with his problem on the team. What we are discussing here is a "transferable" ability. Because ECT relies on authentic feelings, which are simple and easy to learn, the client has a much better chance of utilizing his "learned behavior" with future relationships and events in his life.

One of the most important dynamics of learning Emotional Core Therapy is the wisdom to know that traumatic grief and fear can happen to anyone. Whether one is a master at ECT or just an emotionally healthy person, we all have to live in the real world where loved ones get sick, we argue with parents, flunk a test, etc. For this very reason, it is important to equip yourself with psychological assistance that will help you over a lifetime, and not just once. With ECT, the client is empowered by the process as he is learning it in his long-term memory. He/she will own the technique.

Therapy can be an expensive process. It can hurt to shell out dollar after dollar every time you have a serious relationship issue – and you don't want to have to spend the rest of your adult life in a therapist's office! Why not become your own therapist? When you have learned ECT you can transfer this skill set to all of your relationships, wherever you go, whomever you are with. This is because ECT is fundamentally sound. In the example above, Benny has resolved the difficulty with his girlfriend and coach using ECT. Now Benny can use what he has learned in other fearful events. For example, learning how to scuba dive or explore caves, or overcoming his fear of snakes. Fear is fear, no matter what the relationship is that is causing Benny to feel debilitated. He can steer away from more fearful and grief stricken relationships because he can sense their danger. The more he can distance himself from debilitating feelings, the more powerful he can be in life with his relationships.

Another hypothetical example of how Emotional Core Therapy can help young couples involves a couple named Jared and Kayla. They both had just graduated high school and now they had the entire summer in front of them to do whatever they wanted. Jared's idea was to spend most of his time with his friends, skateboarding, riding dirt bikes and doing other "guy stuff." However, this didn't go over well with Kayla, who felt that now that they were both 18 and high school graduates, they should devote more time to each other. Neither had planned to go to college, but Kayla was going to school to be a medical assistant and she strongly believed that Jared should get some job training too and tried to push him into doing so. Clearly, they didn't see things eye to eye.

Couples therapy would reveal that Jared was resentful of change. He did not like the idea that his relationship with

CHAPTER FIVE

Kayla had to change too. Before when they were in high school, they basically only went out together on dates on weekends and Jared was fine with keeping things that way. But Kayla was not. As we had mentioned previously, nobody can predict the future. If they were going to save their relationship they would have to work towards making Kayla happy. After all, it wasn't fair for only one of them to be happy, nor would their relationship be able to survive that way. This meant that Jared would have to make changes to his plans for the summer. In some manner Jared would have to "grieve" the loss of an unlimited amount of hanging out with his guy friends and just taking it easy.

For Kayla's part, she wanted to stay with Jared if he became a full partner in the relationship. Now that she was becoming more mature, Kayla had grown more confident in herself and her life. She had decided that if he didn't wake up and spend more time with her, she was going to leave him. Fortunately for both of them, the fear of breaking up was a motivating factor. That was in reality something that neither of them wanted.

Using ECT, Jared and Kayla's therapist would make a list each week of the things that Kayla wanted to do and Jared would be encouraged to work hard towards many of these things. It was not the post-graduation life he had envisioned. He had to grieve that loss. He had to process that and recognize that he had to alter certain circumstances of his life that involved reconnecting with his girlfriend.

Initially he had a lot of fear about this, i.e., spending more time with Kayla. For a long time he had avoided her during work but once he had lived with that fear he would then be able to work toward overcoming it on a daily basis. This process might take several months, but eventually they should begin to experience a stronger, more intimate relationship that was no longer teetering on the brink of disaster.

One of the many positive aspects of Emotional Core Therapy is the ability to simplify "psychological help" so that a large sector of the population can benefit from it and use it in their daily life. Earlier in the book we discussed the prevalence of mental health problems. Inappropriate behaviors or inadequate self-soothing techniques cause many of these problems. ECT is a learned process. It relies on using your logic to learn a sequence of steps. ECT also requires you to monitor your body on a daily basis. Most Kindergartens in the United States and around the world follow similar routines. For example, learning the alphabet and following school rules. Most religions also require learning similar training. For example, reciting prayers and following rituals. There is a track record of early intervention in our educational system. So I am optimistic of ECT helping our youth. The key is making mental health a priority.

In closing, let's return to the analogy of the rudderless rowboat one more time, to see what it is that slows a person down in life. Too much water in the rowboat will slow or stop the power. Water inside the rowboat for months and

CHAPTER FIVE

years will make even a "Mercedes" rowboat travel like a paddleboat. We can see what drains the passion out of a strong person's will. It is toxic relationships that cause one to have debilitating feelings of grief and fear for long periods of time. Remember, we can all get "stuck" in hard to deal with relationships from time to time. The key, however, is to diligently apply all that you have learned about Emotional Core Therapy and keep working to find a resolution. Be determined to make whatever changes are necessary to your self-soothing techniques to try and stay calm.

List Five Ways A Couple Can Relax Together

A) GOING ON A PICNIC

B) TAKING A LONG BIKE RIDE ON A NATURE TRAIL

1.
2.
3.
4.
5.

Notes:

5 Step ECT Flow Chart

Relationships; self, other people, places, things

⇩

Four Authentic Feelings; joy, grief, fear, relief

⇩

Uncomfortable Symptoms; muscle tightness, fatigue, etc.

⇩

Releasing Process; learn to discharge toxic feelings

⇩

Balancing Your Equilibrium; practice various daily meditative techniques

CHAPTER SIX
ECT for Advanced Adolescents

Emotional Core Therapy is a form of "self-care" that can help you deal with and overcome life's problems. The goal of this chapter is to tie together everything that you have learned so far in this book, along with some new steps that will provide you with the maximum benefits that Emotional Core Therapy has to offer.

Be patient with the process. It takes time, energy, and resources to learn about the world around you as you continue to grow and develop from an adolescent to an older teenager to a young adult. A good deal of training and education is required to truly understand how best to interact with others. That only makes sense of course. Think about the training involved to be a mechanic or hairstylist. Both take at least a year to become fully licensed. Why? There are lots of important steps to learn to help fix car engines or to give someone's hair a makeover. Fortunately, going to a local mechanic or hair stylist is easy (even though paying for it might not be so easy!). That means that most people will never need to learn the fundamentals of these important trades for themselves.

But it's very different when we're talking about human emotions. The four authentic feelings happen to all of us throughout the day whether we like it or not. The vast majority of us get a little sad or fearful on a weekly basis. At least once a year, a quarter of the population will suffer debilitating feelings of fear and grief. Is it better to ignore training on emotions and run to the nearest therapist's office every time we are troubled emotionally? I think not. An ounce of prevention is worth a pound of cure. That is what this chapter is all about. We are now going to take all that we have learned about ECT so far and take it one step further. Actually, three steps. As you will see in the flow chart at the end of the chapter, altogether there are eight basic steps to Emotional Core Therapy, and they will help you to be fully engaged in the world around you throughout your life.

Back in that early part of the book we had discussed how ECT can help in the often mentally intense sport of golf. One of the concepts I help golfers understand is that each shot is a separate relationship. Therefore it is important to process your authentic feelings after each shot and remain in a peaceful state before you focus on your next shot. Let's take a look at this for a professional player who is playing a typical hole on a course. He will hit his drive out into the fairway. That is one shot and one relationship. Whatever experience he feels on this shot, he needs to process those feelings. In this case, he is happy with his shot so he has moments of joy. He experiences joy and releases those feelings by looking at the trees and water around him. He gets relaxed again and then prepares for his next shot in the fairway. This time he hits a poor shot into the heavy grass around the green, called the "rough". Our golfer is sad for a few minutes, but learns to release the feelings properly by processing his thoughts with his caddie. He then prepares for his next shot, which is called a chip. His ball lies deep down in the grass so he has some excess fear in his mind prior to the shot. He appropriately pays attention to his feelings of fear and changes his routine to accommodate the tough "lie or slope" of the grass. He then plays the shot and hits a nice shot hear the hole. He is quite "relieved" as he now has an easy putt to get his par and do well on the hole. His relief comes from ending a fearful event or relationship.

In my experience, golfers are some of the most stable professional athletes out there. Why? Golf requires not only power but finesse and a soft touch. The game also is filled with human emotions of fear and grief every round. You cannot take drugs or be unstable and be a high performing golfer for a prolonged period of time.

Whether it is on the golf course, or in any other aspect of life, ECT is about gaining the power and independence to choose a healthy lifestyle. It is a viable solution to fighting debilitating feelings of fear and loss because of its exacting nature. All stress comes from entering and leaving relationships. The root cause of stress is moving towards relationships that we like or dislike. One of the key advanced features of ECT is learning how to manage the relationship demands of others. Most relationships require us to meet demands. To keep things simple, we can categorize these into four areas: emotional, financial, spiritual, and physical. Using our five senses (hearing, touching, seeing, tasting, and smelling) we feel one of four ways: joyful, sad, fearful, or relieved. These four feelings can cause our mind and body various levels of discomfort. We have to release these foreign feelings to reach our normal state of relaxation/comfort. Relaxation and comfort need to be reached on a daily basis so we can continually identity foreign feelings (joy, grief, fear, and relief) and deal with them appropriately.

A therapist often acts like a parent figure to his clients. As we said earlier in the book, Mom and Dad always remind their children to dress warmly during the winter for a very good reason. Protection. It is their job to engrain in your mind and your habits the importance of physically protecting yourself to stay healthy and away from harm (such as coming down with pneumonia or getting frostbite). It's very similar to the way in which a therapist wants to help you to maintain your mental health. Of course, you can't go through life with a therapist sitting by your side, which is why Emotional Core Therapy is all about empowering yourself to understand your own emotions and how best to process them. Whether you like it or not, you will suffer fear and loss in your life. In fact,

CHAPTER SIX

most of us will have at least some minor irritation on a daily or weekly basis. I am not a pessimistic person at all, but as a realist I know that your generation is facing some serious global economic problems that have evolved over the past few years. Many people have suffered greatly from traumatic states of fear and grief because of this and other major headaches, but it is all part of the reality of the adult world that you are quickly entering.

Just like everybody else, those who know and practice ECT will still have problems. But they will have a method for dealing with their problems that makes our often-difficult world seem that much more enjoyable. There is a bright side of life that goes beyond our difficulties, and those who know ECT find it easier to get there. One of the many positive aspects of Emotional Core Therapy is the ability to simplify "psychological help" so that virtually anyone can learn the techniques. Look at the alternative. Inappropriate behaviors or inadequate self-soothing techniques cause people all kinds of stress and heartache.

Of course, ECT is a learned process. It relies on using your logic to learn a sequence of steps. ECT also requires you to monitor your body on a daily basis. The training is based on large part on repetition. Practice makes perfect. Most Kindergartens in the United States and around the world follow similar routines. For example, learning the alphabet and following school rules. Most religions also employ similar training. For example, reciting prayers and following rituals.

These are things that remain with you for life – and ECT can become an engrained (permanent) part of your life too.

My goal is for you to master the ECT process by the time you finish reading this book. To help you out even more I would like to point out that the eight-step ECT flowchart is easier to master than meets the eye. Why? The first three steps, whether we like them or not, are constant features of everybody's life on a daily basis. The first three steps are:

1) Understanding the impact that relationships have on our mind and body.

2) Understanding the needs (emotional, financial, spiritual, and physical) of people that we have a relationship with.

3) Having our five senses (hearing, touching, tasting, smelling, and seeing) prompt us to experience one of the four authentic feelings.

Let's look at an example to prove our point. We hear an ambulance race past us down the street with loud sirens blaring. Whether we like it or not we have entered into a relationship that causes us to use our sense of hearing to move out of the way (moving out of the way is a physical need being required of us). When it comes to our visual sense, the sight of a person that we like could bring us to experience the authentic feeling of joy, and conversely touching an oven door that is hot makes us experience fear, so that we literally move away from it. For most of us, such basic tenets of ECT will not be hard to grasp. The real challenge in learning ECT is to identify which authentic feeling is being aroused by your senses. In the case of the ambulance, it is "fear".

The next key learning technique is to monitor your body (messages are constantly being sent to your central nervous system almost unconsciously) and muscular skeletal system for adverse reactions and debilitating symptoms. What kinds of physical reactions are we talking about? It could be things such as goose bumps, chills, sweating, blushing, muscles tensing up, teeth grinding, etc. There are all kinds of physical reactions that your central nervous system is "hard wired" to respond with when various stimuli come to your brain through your five senses.

This is common to all human beings of all ages and from every culture currently or previously on the face of the Earth. Increased heart rate and breathing when a person is scared, for example, comes from the "fight or flight" instinct that kept our distant ancestors alive when they lived in very hostile environments with large predatory animals that constantly threatened them. A rush of adrenaline accompanied by these other physical reactions would give them the extra edge that they needed to either defeat or to flee potential adversaries, either animal or human. Today, our circumstances usually aren't that severe, but the basic concepts and, perhaps more importantly our bodies are pretty much the same. Therefore, when you get really nervous and your heart is racing when you have to get up and read an essay in front of the whole class, you can thank your ancient ancestors for those sweaty palms and tense shoulders!

Fortunately, one of the really cool things about Emotional Core Therapy is that it works *with* your senses and your central nervous system rather than against them. ECT doesn't deny that you will have negative energy throughout your life, or try to wish it away, but instead it teaches you to learn how to release it.

We had also mentioned the importance of learning to meet the various demands of people we are in relationships with. Let's briefly look at each of these:

Emotional: Just as you want to be emotionally healthy (which is what ECT is all about) your actions and behaviors will affect the emotional needs of those around you. For example, your parents want to feel secure that you are safe and happy. You can meet this emotional need that they have by showing them that you are maturing at a good pace and becoming a responsible young person. This will very much help to put their mind at ease.

Financial: Even teenagers have an impact on the financial needs of others, though perhaps not as much as adults. Sure, you probably don't have a family to support, but you are at the age where what you do impacts the financial needs of others. For example, can you help your family with college costs by working part-time? Also, by studying hard you can earn scholarship money that can also help ease the financial demands on your parents.

CHAPTER SIX

Spiritual: When you think about it, spirituality is ageless. You could be 15 or 95, when it comes to eternal spiritual things those numbers don't mean very much. We are all the same. Human beings experience all kinds of spiritual states. You may have a friend, for example, who is at a very low point in his life. He can't see beyond the misery of his current circumstances. You can lift him out of the spiritual doldrums just by being a good listener. In other words, just by being there for him as a good friend you are helping to fulfill his spiritual needs.

Physical: Oftentimes people mistake "physical" for "sexual," and although that can be a part of it, meeting the physical needs of others covers much more than just intimacy. It can also mean, for example, helping a friend who is trying to get into shape. Or it might mean keeping your little sister safe when she is outside playing by keeping a close eye on her. There are all kinds of ways that you can help with the physical needs of the people in your life.

Emotional Core Therapy teaches us that a diligent effort to maintain peace and relaxation is needed to remind the body of its normal state of comfort. For nearly all of us, it will take a few months at the very least to master these techniques. This only makes sense, because we are retraining our mind and body, which takes time and effort. Nothing comes easy, but the reward of a healthy and balanced lifestyle is well worth the effort.

Make no mistake about it, you don't want to underestimate the time and work involved in understanding and utilizing

Emotional Core Therapy. It sometimes takes between two and eight months to get full relief from debilitating feelings of grief and fear. Over the years I have seen many people who desire a quick fix for emotional issues that have no easy cure. That's not how it normally works. In some cases, there may be no complete solution in the short-term, only partial remedies. This is just as true for adults as it is for teenagers. For example, if a man who is supporting a large family works at a job where he absolutely hates his tyrant of a boss, this would cause him a good deal of anxiety and stress. However, leaving that situation, especially in today's terrible employment environment, probably would not be practical for this man. He could not economically afford it, so he would need to use ECT to come up with at least some partial relief.

You will likely find situations like that in your own life too, not necessarily involving a job, but other things that you have very little control over. Maybe your parents decide to move the family to another part of the country. You're under eighteen so you have no choice but to go along with the move even if you're totally opposed to it. As we all know, that's just the way life is sometimes. Still, ECT will help you to maintain your peace of mind and realize that even things that seem like the biggest problems in the world are manageable when you learn, memorize and practice the right techniques.

The following are hypothetical yet realistic examples of how solving problems can take an extended period of time before seeing any improvement. The first case involves a high

CHAPTER SIX

school junior girl named Abby. One day, Abby suddenly finds that she has to move far away from where she grew up after her dad gets a job transfer to another state. This young lady had built loving and trusting relationships with friends since birth and now she wouldn't be able to see them any longer. This type of grief or loss can take months and maybe a year or so to process and cathartically release the pain. It would be completely unrealistic to just expect her feelings to somehow magically change overnight.

Another example would be a high school sophomore boy, Kyle, whose father is dying of cancer. In all likelihood Kyle would face fear and grief for a year or two on a daily basis. His suddenly secure world is changing for the worse, and it must feel like everything is crumbling around him. This type of tragic situation of course takes a good deal of time and work to understand and cope with to resolve.

A third situation would be a high school freshman girl, Lexi, who gets overly ambitious and takes too many hard classes for her first year in high school. The demands she faces cause excess fear from September to June of her school year. Her problem is deep, and not likely to quickly disappear.

All three of these examples are very typical of the kinds of things that can and do happen to many high school adolescents. There is no cure for these emotional issues but having a good support system in place is an important piece of the puzzle. In fact, it is indispensable. A good support system would help each one of these emotionally bothered kids to identify and process their feelings. Ultimately, this would help to bring joy into their lives.

It is also very important, actually it is absolutely essential, to mediate daily. Don't confuse this with some kind of chanting or religious ritual (unless that is what works for you). By meditation, I am referring more broadly to allowing your mind to daydream, wander and reflect. Not only is this practice very beneficial for your mental health, but it also allows you to cathartically release pent up feelings. Throughout this book we have given lots of examples of things that people can do that can help them meditate such as yoga, soaking in a jacuzzi, taking a walk, etc. The goal with all of this is to learn to monitor, identify and release the four authentic feelings, which are temporary states of being. The peace and stability that this can bring to your life is immeasurable.

One of the best ways to banish depression from your thinking is to concentrate and spend time on the things that bring you joy. A therapist using ECT will often ask his client to search their memories for specific times when they were happy. What were they doing? What did it involve? What do they remember about it that they liked so much. The list for each person might look very different. For example, this could be Abby's list:

1. Spending an afternoon at the spa
2. Riding her bike
3. Listening to music in her bedroom
4. Painting with watercolors

CHAPTER SIX

5. Shopping for new clothes
6. Writing poetry
7. Walking the dog
8. Looking at old pictures in a photo album
9. Baking cookies and other stuff with her mom
10. Watching game shows on TV

Kyle's list, on the other hand, could include these top ten things that bring him joy:

1. Snowboarding
2. Playing chess
3. Swimming
4. Building model airplanes
5. Lifting weights
6. Practicing guitar
7. Playing video games
8. Going to church on Sunday mornings
9. Reading comic books
10. Watching sports on TV

Lexi would have her own list. Since we are all individuals, she may or may not share some of the same or similar items on her list, which only makes sense since we are all human yet each one of us is unique.

This would be the list of the top ten things that bring Lexi joy:

1. Taking a bubble bath
2. Playing Frisbee with her dog

3. Shopping
4. Working out in front of an aerobics video on TV
5. Chatting on the phone about boys with her friends
6. Visiting with her grandparents
7. Jogging
8. Reading old diary entries from when she was younger
9. Playing basketball with her little brother
10. Reading celebrity magazines

What about your list? No matter how many down times we might have in life, never forget about all of those things that bring you happiness. My hope is that what you have learned in this book will make you realize just how much power you have to control your own life and your own destiny. You are only young once and you should enjoy the ride for all it's worth.

Once you have read this book from cover to cover, you can then assess how much knowledge you have attained learning the ECT process. If you can only recall six of the eight steps, for example, you can then focus on learning the remaining two steps, without having to reread the whole book. The important thing is to know that, like life itself, ECT is an ongoing process. This book will always be there for you to refer back to, but as time goes by you will find more and more that you do not need to keep reading it. That's because Emotional Core Therapy will empower you to help yourself. It shows you a healthy way of life that never runs away from being human, but instead fully embraces it.

CHAPTER SIX

ECT Flow Chart

Relationships; self, other people, places, things

⬇

Needs; emotional, financial, spiritual, physical

⬇

Five Senses; seeing, touching, smelling, tasting, hearing

⬇

Four Authentic Feelings; joy, grief, fear, relief

⬇

Effects; brain/central nervous system

⬇

Uncomfortable Symptoms; muscle tightness, fatigue, etc.

⬇

Releasing Process; learn to discharge toxic feelings

⬇

Balancing Your Equilibrium; practice various daily meditative techniques